The Elevator to The Top:

Your Go-To Resource for All Things Sales

Ryan Stewman

Table of Contents

HARDCORE RESOURCES

Facebook
125,000 followers
Fan: https://www.facebook.com/HardcoreCloser/
Group: https://www.facebook.com/groups/salestalk/
Personal: https://www.facebook.com/realryanstewman

Twitter
10,000 followers
Personal: https://twitter.com/ryanstewman
Business: https://twitter.com/hardcorecloser

LinkedIn
6,000 followers
Personal: https://www.linkedin.com/in/ryanstewman
Business: http://www.linkedin.com/co/hardcorecloser

Instagram
20,000 followers
Personal: https://www.instagram.com/ryanstewman/
Business: https://www.instagram.com/hardcorecloser/

#43 Business Podcast on iTunes, 3,000 subscribers
https://itunes.apple.com/us/podcast/ the-hardcore-
closer-podcast/id1098856846?mt=2

YouTube
1.5 million views
https://www.youtube.com/user/ryanstewman

Clyxo
www.Clyxo.com/Closer

Snapchat
ryanstewman

Skype
ryanstewman

Blog
400,000 Visitors Monthly
Sales Talk For Sales Pros
www.HardcoreCloser.com
Articles, Digital Products, Training Resources

Books

- *Bulletproof Business: Protect Yourself Against The Competition (2016)*
- *Kick Ass - Take Names, Emails and Phone Numbers (2015)*
- *Hardcore [c]loser, **A Top Business Book of all time, Amazon (Best Seller)** (2015)*

Chapter 1

Seven Reasons Salespeople Have the Best Job on the Planet

I took my first sales job at the ripe age of thirteen. I had been working at the same car wash company since I was eight years old. I started mowing their yard, and at age 12 they let me vacuum cars. Mowing the grounds and vacuuming cars is no joke in 100-degree Texas heat. While working the vacuums, I noticed the guy who sold the washes to the customers got to stay in the shade all day. This was very appealing to me.

After paying closer attention, I also realized the salesman didn't vacuum or wash cars. He literally had the easiest job on the lot. It was in that moment I knew I was going to be a salesman. A year later, I made it a reality. Funny thing is, I had to really sell myself as a 13-year old capable of communicating to adults. When I closed the boss on it, I proved I was worthy.

Since that moment, I've been 100 percent convinced salespeople have the best job on the planet. Nowhere else can you make your own rules, your own money and do your own thing. In sales, it happens every day. I've made a list of the top seven reasons working in sales is where it's at.

#1: We Make Our Own Rules

Name another job where you can come and go as you please. I'm pretty sure there's no other position where the employee is above management's rules either. If you're a good salesman, you can tell the manager to kiss your ass and they just might have to do it.

When I worked at Texas Lending, casual Friday was the only day you could wear jeans. I wore jeans every day and even the CEO never said anything. Why? Because I made them $50-100 grand every month. Therefore, they let me make my own rules. It's a pleasure only top dogs can experience.

#2: We Have No Income Ceiling

I don't know about you, but I don't want anyone telling me what I'm worth. I don't allow another single person to place value on my worth. Instead, I'll go out and prove my value to multiple people. I'm the type of person, who, if you put a limit on my income, I'll put a limit on the production I give you.

Earning what you are worth is way more fun than settling for a salary. Let the salaries go to the people who are afraid to take risks and live by a budget. We salespeople can blow all our money on Friday and make it all back on Monday. Take that HR!

#3: Our Clients Love Us

One thing I love about sales is there are other departments that deal with complaints. The only time we hear from our clients is when they thank us and tell us how much they love what we sold them. We don't have to do anything but solve problems and close.

When you're a Grade A problem solver, your clients love you. Who doesn't love someone who helped them fix an issue? If there's a problem, they

still don't complain to us. They take it out on the operations and support staff.

#4: Our Employers Love Us

When you make the person or company you work for a lot of money, they love you. It's simple math. You + Sales = Happy Employer. Yeah, the boss may have taken Dorothy from accounting to lunch that *one time* she uncovered a huge error that saved the company, but he'll take someone in sales out often.

I've never seen a manager or CEO walk into a company and high five the operations department. I *have* seen them take shots at 10am with the sales team, though!

#5: We Travel Often

When you've got the killer instinct and the company knows it, they want you to be the face of the enterprise any chance you get. This means when they have meetings, events, conventions and the like, you're the go-to person. If they know you can sell, they will send you to tell.

They can't send Dorothy and Harold off to some convention as the face. They need a salesperson to do that. Nobody buys from the accounting department. So, Harold and Dorothy can just stay behind at the office, while we salesmen handle the big boy business.

#6: We Meet New People Constantly

If you're in sales and you're not a people person, you're not really in sales. You have to know and like people in order to sell to them. By liking people, I mean the idea of bonding and solving another human's problem. Every day, we are looking for new people to meet. From cold calls to networking events to inbound leads, we are constantly meeting and helping new, cool people.

A good salesman knows that when you meet people, you ask those new people to introduce you to more people...AND repeat. New people are key to growing a sales pipeline. Getting to learn more people's stories is exciting to most of us. It's a blast to help someone with a problem and then convert them from stranger to client.

#7: We Have Connections Everywhere

No one calls Harold in HR when they need a hook-up somewhere. They call the guys down in the sales department for that. All those new people I mentioned previously come with connections—who are eager to help a salesman.

Plus, everyone wants to know a salesman they can trust. They know trustworthy salespeople also have other trustworthy salespeople in their network. When I was a LO, people asked me to connect them with car people, clubs and pretty much anything. They knew I knew people, that the people I knew were good.

How much do you love your job in sales? What if you made even more money at your job? If you made more money would you be more excited to go to work every day? What could you do in order to increase your income? One action to take is to educate yourself and learn new stuff. I recommend you check out www.showupandclose.com and learn fresh ways to close more sales and increase your income.

If you're ready to invest in your personal success

and you'd like to find out about the programs we have developed especially for you, simply head over to www.HardcoreCloser.com/tribe and we'll have a sales conversation about your future.

Chapter 2

10 Easy Ways to Save Money When Starting Out at a New Sales Job

I remember when I took my first corporate sales job, slinging mortgages. I was broke AF when I walked in the door. Prior to that, I had been selling car washes for around $10.50/hour. I couldn't afford to be there and I couldn't afford to screw it up. I had to get good with money quick.

The same thing happened to me in 2008. I had just gotten out of federal prison for firearms charges ('Merica) and while inside, my (ex) wife had left me for the gardener. She had also taken all my cash and assets. I had nothing but one option left: my *new job*. I looked at it as my last chance, one I couldn't afford to blow.

All OG salespeople have been there. We've all started at the bottom at some point. Allow me to do the OG thing and hook you up with some knowledge on how you can save some cash while you're in a tight spot, building your pipeline. Here are 10 easy ways to save money when starting out at a new sales job:

#1: Download Smart Phone Apps

When you start out at a new job, it seems as if you always need to buy something technological. Software, devices, or whatever. It all varies from company to company. Most of the products that cost quite a bit of money can be found for as low as ninety-nine cents or even for free on your smart phone. Check your phone store before you buy anywhere else.

#2: Advertise Online Instead of Buying Paper and Toner

These days, you don't need to get business cards, print flyers or any of that. Thanks to social media and sites like Craigslist, you can do all the advertising and prospecting you need to do, online and paper-free. Toner is one of the most expensive office supplies on the planet. Save the cash by going online and marketing there.

#3: Split Costs with a Coworker

Most likely, there's someone else new in the office who's just as broke as you. Hook up with that person and agree to split some of the higher costs involved in doing your job. Maybe even divide the cost of an online marketing campaign.

#4: Use the Company's Materials

The company has swag, marketing materials and

stuff you need. Don't reinvent the wheel and think you have to have something cooler. Save the cash. Use the materials the company provides. Even use their paper and toner, if needed. Use anything the company supplies instead of going out and buying your own. You can get your own later when you close some sales. For now, make do with what you have available.

#5: Network Online to Save Gas and Food Money

Food and gas are the most expensive parts of starting a new sales job, especially if you have to drive around and buy prospects' lunches. It can add up quick. Networking meetings don't take place at Wendy's. You can blow 20 or 30 bucks at one single networking lunch, and that's not counting gas money. Network online, eat a sandwich and save your money. These days online and offline networking are equally effective.

#6: Meet Prospects at Your Office

As I mentioned earlier, gas and food add up quickly, especially when you have to buy for others. Sure, the company may reimburse you, but you may not have time to wait until they do. Meeting prospects at your office saves you from having to buy anything. It also gets the prospect on your turf, so you have a better chance of closing the deal—bonus!

#7: Only Go to Networking Events with Free Food

Similar to the gas and food equation, also stay up to date on the free food spots. I had a friend who knew every spot in town that offered free appetizers for each day of the week. He only went to events with free food. He didn't buy dinner, but like five times a year! This can save you $100+ weekly.

#8: Drink Only Water at Happy Hour Meet-ups

You may think I'm being insane here, but let's get real. If you don't have much money, the last thing you need to do is drink. If you're broke, you don't need to celebrate. Save the money and get some sales closed. Also, if you're sober and your guests are buzzed, you'll have the closing advantage over them. People agree to the best stuff when under the influence. Let that happen to them, not you.

#9: Take Your Lunch to Work

Saving 10 to 20 dollars each day by taking your lunch is a no-brainer. Between saving on lunch and the networking events sponsoring your dinner each night, you can save at least 50 bucks. That 50 bucks can go toward things you do need, like marketing campaigns, and other materials that will generate more sales for you. Taking your lunch to work is easy. In 2008, I ate sandwiches and chips every day for three months while I built my empire.

#10: Use Public Transportation

I live in Dallas where we have an awesome rail situation. If you can take public transportation to work, do it. Trains here are filled with all sorts of people. Besides saving money on a car and gas, you can also talk to new people and possibly run into a few new prospects. You're a salesman, in the middle of a lot of people. Surely, by doing this enough, you'll get a sale somewhere.

Starting out broke in a commission-only job can be tough. If you'll stick with it though, there is light on the other side. In 2008, I was broke AF and now I'm not. Matter of fact, by the end of 2008, I wasn't broke any more. I went from eating sandwiches for lunch each day to dining at the best restaurants in the area. It just took discipline, determination and patience to make it happen. You can do the same. Stay the course. If you want to fast track your success, invest in www.inboundleadcloser.com and you won't be broke for long!

If you're ready to invest in your personal success and you'd like to find out about the programs we have developed especially for you, simply head over to www.HardcoreCloser.com/tribe and we'll have a sales conversation about your future.

Chapter 3

Five Personality Traits You Must Possess to Be an Effective Salesman

It's obvious sales is NOT for everyone. Most salesmen aren't closing deals and are starving to death. We ALL know how it is: someone says you'd be good in sales; you need a job, and the next thing you know you're trying to make deals. To make matters worse, most of the time the person hiring isn't a salesperson either, so they have no clue what to look for in a new hire.

Just think of how many prospects are out there, wandering around, still looking to get closed, because the salesman they happen to cross paths with couldn't close a screen door on a windy day. I've gone behind my fair share of lost deals and turned them back into sales. People always ask me how I do it. It just comes naturally. In sales, you've either got it or you don't.

The key is to know what to look for. Why waste your time and income in a sales position if it's not for you? You're going to need a few key personality traits if you want to collect big commission checks. If you're not born with these traits, you must learn and develop them. Without 'em you can't close shit.

None of these traits are greater than the other. They are codependent on each other. There's no replacing or making up for them either. Just remember, we are not born with traits. They can be learned, implemented and become habitual. It's not that hard to adapt this personality. Naturally, everyone is going to have one or two of these traits, but very few will have all five. Those possessing all five are the Closers.

#1: Good Listener

The person who talks the least makes the most. As salesmen, we are looking for a problem from the prospect, so we can provide a probable solution. When people are telling you about their problems they tend to talk a lot. A good salesman has to genuinely care, be empathetic and listen to the prospect. If you're not a good listener, you lose. No one wants to hear a sales pitch; they want to hear a solution pitch.

These days, people forget a person's name seconds after they introduce themselves. The guys and gals who listen to others really stand out. When you listen to someone, you show you care. People enjoy buying from people who actually care. There are plenty of people who don't give a shit out there. Most salesmen talk too much. The way to close is with your ears, not your mouth.

#2: *Friendly as a Box of Kittens*

If you don't like strangers or if you're scared to meet new people, you'll never make it in sales. Just know this: the sales you make will come from strangers. The people who know you well rarely buy from you. I know this is the opposite of what most sales managers teach, but it's the truth. Ego and vulnerability are to blame for this. It is what it is. The sooner you realize it, the sooner you can sell to strangers.

You'd be surprised how many sales are made due to a smile. People like buying from friendly people. Meeting strangers and exchanging money can create some awkward situations. The friendlier you are, the less time you spend in the awkward zone. Treating prospects like longtime friends will get you a lot of sales. Most people's friends don't even treat them like friends.

#3: *Fast Thinker*

If you're going to make big money in sales, you've got to be sharp. If you're like me, you've got to work and practice harder than the next guy. Learning every single detail about what you sell helps. When the prospect throws out objections or questions, you've got to be quick with the answer. Quick answers scream confidence. Slow, thought-out answers show inexperience.

Fast thinkers are decision makers. One of the hardest things to do is to get a human to make a decision. When you demonstrate your ability to make fast decisions, others get a sense of confidence from you. Confidence sells products. Plus, you've got to be sharp when the client is throwing you zinger objections and trying to crawfish out of a sale.

#4: People Pleaser

Sales is all about making people happy by selling them what they want/need. If you don't like to put smiles on folks' faces, sales isn't for you. You've got to truly want to see prospects happy and satisfied or you'll never make it. People can tell by your face and body language if you like them or not. People don't like paying money to people who don't like them.

When people buy stuff, they want to feel good about it. If you genuinely care about them, they can tell. When people come to you with their problems and they see you really want to help them, they want to pay you. The more prospects you please, the bigger your check will be. Happy people and closed sales go hand in hand.

#5: Thick-skinned

I saved this one for last because it's more about

them than it is about you. The previous four traits pertain to you; this trait pertains to you, but is about them. Salesmen are shit on often. People don't particularly care for us. Knowing this, you've got to be able to take the good with the bad. When it comes to buying, some will, some won't. So what? Every time you're in a situation where the prospect isn't cool, you have to remember the other times when they were.

If you're not able to take criticism, sarcasm and berating from time to time, you're not cut out for sales. In a business where the customer is right 99 percent of the time, you have to be willing to take it in the shorts and own up when it's on you. The good news is that after a while, you get used to it and none of the BS matters.

If you'll conjure up and use all five of these traits to your advantage, you'll end up closing a lot more deals with a lot happier prospects. When I sold cars and had to greet someone on the lot, I always ran over to them, enthusiastically welcomed them and then asked their story. Most of my colleagues had a ho-hum approach and it was blatantly obvious which worked better.

If you're in sales and you get fresh leads on a daily basis, whether from the Internet or walk ups, I've got a program that when combined with the above five personality traits can take you from good to great. The program is called Ultimate Inbound Lead Selling System and you can get the first video free at www.inboundleadcloser.com.

If you're ready to invest in your personal success and you'd like to find out about the programs we have developed especially for you, simply head to www.HardcoreCloser.com/tribe and we'll have a sales conversation about your future.

Chapter 4

The Difference Between Salespeople and Sales Closers

Just because you can sell, doesn't mean you can close. Selling is useless if you can't close. The money is not made in the sell; it's made in the close. Being a sales person is one thing. Being a sales closer is another. Closers have a unique ability to see things to the end. When the objections start to rise, salespeople flinch. Not closers; they stay in the sell until it's closed.

Here's One of the Most Common Mistakes Made in the Sales Industry:

Business owner, Bob is out to eat at a nice restaurant. Bob has a waiter named Kyle. Kyle is attentive, witty, funny and has a great personality. Bob says, "You know Kyle, you'd do well in sales," and offers him a job. Wanting to get away from $2.12/hour, Kyle accepts the job. After a month or two, Bob starts to scratch his head as to why Kyle can't close.

This happens all the time. The thing is, waiters, waitresses and service industry people don't sell. They take orders. They simply ask you what YOU want, and then they go get it for you. When's the last time you went to a restaurant and ordered something, then were upsold to something completely different? Never, that's when. Order takers aren't closers.

Just because you have a good attitude, look nice and can talk a little doesn't mean you can close shit. Closing is not about looks, talking, or attitude. It's about being fearless of rejections. Sales closers are not afraid to hear the word "no." The guys and girls who can close deals do so with thick skin and an agenda to handle their business.

There's a Big Difference Between Sales People and Sales Closers

Anyone can work in sales. Job openings pop up every day. Check Glassdoor.com, Craigslist and any other listing site for plenty of sales openings. Every one of these job listings asks for sales people. I've never seen a job post searching for sales closers.

All it takes to work in sales is a good attitude and a willingness to work commission-only. Being a closer takes patience, practice and persistence. Closers stay in the sale until it's done. In this world of ADD and unfinished projects, closers don't move on until the job they are doing is done. Closers finish what they start.

Salespeople tend to give up on the first or second

objection. They worry the prospect may not like them and may start to judge them for being aggressive. Closers know what they sell is in the best interest of the prospect and they will stop at nothing to push the prospect to make a decision for their own good.

Closers are not afraid to hear "no" and then keep pushing the prospect closer to "Yes!" Closers can remove emotion from the equation and stay in the sell until it's done. Their follow-up is relentless, and their work ethic unreal. Closers keep companies afloat and in the black.

Salespeople are Afraid to Have Hard Conversations and Will Want to Bond with the Prospect More Than Close Them

I'd rather be paid than liked. That's the attitude of a closer. Salespeople don't think that way. They'd rather be liked than paid. It's one thing to provide good service; it's another to get paid for providing good service. If you're going to close sales, you're going to have to make prospects uncomfortable. Salespeople aren't cut out for that part of the job.

I've sold cars, houses and mortgages. In each of those positions, I've seen 10 times as many salespeople as closers. Each month on the leaderboard, you can spot the closer. He's the guy in the number one spot. It's equally as easy to spot salespeople. They are the ones talking to prospects, selling prospects, but not closing shit.

Let me be straight with you. I'm not knocking salespeople. Our industry is based around them. They warm up the prospects for us closers to come in and lock them down. There's a need for both types in our industry, but only one of them makes the big bucks.

If you're a closer, next time someone asks you "What do you do for a living?" instead of saying, "I'm in sales," say "I'm a sales closer." It sets you apart from the rest. Simply having the confidence to present yourself in such a way means you're bold enough to hold the title.

Salespeople can also convert into closers. With enough desire, experience and drive, a salesperson can morph into a closer. Most of us closers started out as salespeople. We worked our way into becoming the sales beasts you see before you. With each turn, we took mental notes from our wins and losses. Eventually, we armed ourselves with enough information to break through to the closer side of sales.

Closing is a skill that's necessary for salespeople to learn. The problem is most salespeople think they are closers, but much like the Maury Povich show, results of their paycheck reveal they are *not* the closer. Take a minute and reflect on your sales style, then ask yourself, "Am I a sales closer or a sales person?" If you're not sure, look at your paycheck.

If you'd like to convert from salesperson to sales closer, I've got the help you need. Closers are committed to learning and improving. If you're going to improve, you're going to need help and experience. Every closer out there took the time to consume information to make them better. Whether that information came from books, mentors, or even sales managers, they had help.

I'd like to offer you help, too. Even if you are a closer, you can always improve. My sales training program www.showupandclose.com will turn even a subpar sales person into a sales closer within six months. By repeatedly learning and memorizing my program, you'll be able to say the effortless and effective words to close those prospects like spring-loaded screen doors.

If you're ready to invest in your personal success and you'd like to find out about the programs we have developed especially for you, simply head over to www.HardcoreCloser.com/tribe and we'll have a sales conversation about your future.

Chapter 5

Seven Common Mistakes Average Salespeople Make

If you've been around the sales game for any amount of time, you've seen your fair share of both green peas and experts blow sales. It's like watching a train wreck. You want to look away; you even want to help, but all you can do is watch. Watching a sale fall to hell is one of the most entertaining parts of our job, as long as it's not our sale.

We always talk like it's only the new guy who's blowing sales, but we've all seen a lot of old heads screwing up deals, too. These are the guys who insist on still using 80's sales tactics while trying to close in 2016. Even the customer sees through their BS from miles away. Losing a sale hurts everyone, though. When the new guy or OG blows a sale, it hurts the reputation of the company, which affects everyone…even the prospect…because they didn't get their problem solved.

In all my years of selling and managing sales people, I've noticed some key common mistakes sales folks make, which cost them sales. I'm going to point out the seven most common things average salespeople do that cost them closes. After reading this, you'll have to take self-inventory and make sure one or more of these habits is not costing you. Here are seven mistakes average salespeople make that cost sales:

#1: Talking Too Much

This is the biggest and most common mistake you can make as a salesman. Yet, it happens all day, every day. Talking too much costs salesmen and businesses billions annually (accurate guess.) I know that the world says, *You're a good talker. You'd make a good salesman.* But, that's usually coming from the mouth of someone not in sales.

The truth is, great salesmen operate in silence, like the "G" in lasagna. A master salesman knows the prospect should say 7-10 words for every word he speaks. If they speak for thirty seconds, you speak for five. Asking questions is the key to getting the prospect to talk. Get them to talk and they'll tell you what to sell them. If you're busy talking too much, they can't get a word in and that word could be "sold," but you'd never know.

#2: Not Knowing the Product

If you're not asking the prospect questions, they're asking you. If you don't know the ins and outs of what you sell, you're done. Without proper product knowledge, the prospect will think, *I like it, but this guy knows nothing about it. I need to make sure it solves my problem*. They won't buy due to lack of certainty.

You owe it to your prospects, your company and yourself to know every detail about what you sell as well as every angle in which to sell it. Only average people wing it when it comes to work. To be an exceptional and master salesperson, you have to know every feature of your product or service, inside and out. Prospects rely on you for answers. If you don't have the answers, they won't have the confidence to buy.

#3: Don't Believe in What They Are Selling

When I sold cars, I drove what I sold. I knew if I was going to be a top producer, I had to be bought in. I wanted to experience what the client would experience. I wanted to look at them in the eye and tell them I made the same buying decision recently and that I was happy. Any service questions, equipment questions or otherwise, I had answers for them firsthand, because I'd sold myself first. *I* was my first sale.

Most people don't, and won't use what they sell. It's sad. Salespeople wonder why they aren't selling a lot of product, only to realize they're selling something they don't believe in and wouldn't buy themselves. It's hard to convince someone to do something you wouldn't do without using the phrase: "I dare you!"

#4: Overcomplicate the Process

Ever heard the phrase "Keep It Simple Stupid" before? It's probably the most well-known, yet ignored lesson in sales. Just because you know everything about the product and process doesn't mean the prospect has to hear it. When the double helix was discovered, and the scientist was awarded the Nobel Peace Prize, it took him five minutes only to explain the entire presentation. If it takes more than five minutes to explain what you sell, you're overcomplicating the process.

These days, people have short attention spans. When you overcomplicate the interaction (talking too much: see #1), you lose the prospect's attention. When I sold mortgages, if I had tried to explain the bond market and how interest rates worked I would have never closed a single deal. Instead I always said, "Low rates? Got 'em!" I kid you not; I sold thousands of mortgages using that phrase.

#5: Selling the Product, Not the Results

No one wants a mortgage. What they want is a house. The mortgage is merely a hurdle in-between what they have and what they want. Sell the house. Not the mortgage. When I sold mortgages, I watched dudes struggle all day long trying to sell interest rates. Meanwhile, I was crushing it selling houses. Ultimately, we both sold the same product, but I sold results: homeownership.

Think of it this way. No one wants a drill. What they want is a hole. Find the hole and fill it. That's the way of a true salesman. Average salespeople pitch products. Master salespeople sell results.

#6: Appreciating the Prospect's Time

When a salesperson says, "Thanks for your time," or "I really appreciate you taking the time with me today," you insinuate the prospect's time is worth more than yours. You give them a dominance frame you will struggle to come back from. Thanking a customer for their time is like asking about the weather. It's small talk that's not needed and positions you in the wrong light. Avoid it.

Your time is just as, if not more important, than the prospect's time. Make sure you let them know. My favorite is to push the *rushed sale*. In other words, I let them know up front that I'm busy and this process will be quick. I let them know I'm not here to waste my time or theirs. We're getting this deal done. Now.

#7: Not Following Up

This is the most annoying, yet lucrative part of

sales. Most salespeople simply refuse to follow up. Be it because they have a steady stream of new leads, or maybe they didn't earn the right to follow up. Either way, most salespeople don't follow up and are scared to death to do it.

Meanwhile, over here in Closerland, we call everyone until they tell us not to. Our secret is always calling with a gift. "Hey Ryan, I have a blog post I'd like you to read," or "Hey Ryan, I have a free book for you. Where do you want it sent?" My prospects enjoy the follow up. They know even after they buy, we follow up and make sure they are happy. When you take action, you show you care.

Want to know how to tell if you're an average salesman or not? Look at your check. If you made less than $10,000 in the last month, you're average. You may not want to hear it, but it is what it is. Don't even come at me with the: "You can't make $10,000 a month selling what I sell." There's someone out there doing it, which only reinforces how average you are. The truth will set you free, but it may piss you off first.

If you're ready to take the leap from average to top producer, I've got the all-around best-selling program on the market: my Show Up and Close sales training at www.buyshowupandclose.com. When you make the investment and take action, you'll become the one percent!

If you're ready to invest in your personal success and you'd like to find out about the programs we have developed especially for you, simply head over to www.HardcoreCloser.com/tribe and we'll have a sales conversation about your future.

Chapter 6

Five Dead Giveaways That Tell Prospects You're Desperate for Business

Nothing is worse than appearing like you're a broke ass salesman. One of the keys to closing sales is confidence. It's hard to have confidence when you're broke AF. The problem is, for most of us, when you're broke, you're desperate, and when you're desperate, you struggle to close sales. The prospect can smell fear and desperation from miles away.

A few tell-tale signs prospects (especially good ones) sniff out, can take place right off the bat. The time when you are most likely to make a sale is when you don't need it. The time when you are least likely to make a sale, is when you need it most. No prospect wants to make a deal with a needy salesman. People are closed on confidence; the confidence they have made the right decision. A desperate, needy salesman can't deliver confidence.

The future is here! The same BS sales tactics that worked in the 80's don't work as well these days. Prospects are smarter than ever. They are also busier and more distracted. Thanks to the Internet, most prospects now have a keen sense for detecting desperation, too. High-level executives and entrepreneurs know the difference between a successful salesperson and a needy one.

I'm going to give you five signs that tell prospects you're desperate for business. If you're in hard times and you're making one of these mistakes, stop it. The reason you're having hard times is probably due to one or more of the issues I'm about to share with you. Identify which ones are hurting you, and use the information you learn to overcome them.

#1: You Cold-Call

It's 2016, and according to AT&T, 86-90 percent of ALL phone calls go unanswered. We've added the barriers of caller ID, text messages, the Do Not Call Registry and more, to avoid using the phone with anyone we don't WANT to talk to. Yet, salesmen cold call every day and say, "I've made 300 dials today, but only talked to five people." What a waste of time. At that point, just use an auto dialer.

CEOs, bosses and the real players in every industry know cold calling is low level stuff. They know no one in any position of power is making cold calls. Cold calls are a sign of desperation and no money to market your product properly. Now, I get that if you work on Wall Street and you make a million cold calling, that's an exception. Referrals and advertising are what people who are good and have money use to market themselves. Cold calls reek of neediness.

#2: *You Show Up Unannounced*

Right up front, you appear as if you had nothing better to do because you assumed the prospect had nothing better to do either. Producers are busy. They don't like surprises and they have a schedule to maintain. The very fact you appear as if you don't, makes them think you're needy. If you're selling to the top (which you should be) you should know they have been in your shoes. They know your mindset!

If you're going to sell to the top, you've got to show them you're just as important and busy as they are. Showing up unannounced, then trying to sell them something, won't work. Even when it does, it's a fluke, not a norm. You've got to set a time, show up, let them know you don't have but 20 minutes. Then pitch, close and leave. Always set an appointment first. If you have a secretary, assistant, or coworker who can set the appointment for you, even better.

#3: *You Talk Too Much*

Often, when a salesperson gets a chance to set an appointment, be it on the phone or in person, they talk too much. Worse yet, most people fail to confirm an appointment because they ask for too much time. If you need an hour to pitch your prospect, you talk too damn much. Ask for 10-20 minutes of the prospect's time, max. Let them know you're busy and are limited on time. Hone your pitch into as few words as possible. Keep it short and matter-of-fact.

If the prospect likes what you're saying, they will ask you for more of your time. Then and ONLY then, can you use up an hour of their time. Get good enough to where they ask you for more of your time. This is called a "trial close" and it's definitely a buying sign. Get 'em!

#4: You Thank Them for Their Time

Honestly, I don't care what a prospect does with their time. For all I know, in the minutes I talked to them, I've kept them away from drugs, hookers, or a car accident. Who am I to call it? Joking aside, never thank a prospect for their time. It gives their time superiority over yours. When you're a producer and making a lot of sales, your time is worth just as much or more than the prospects you're pitching. Never make their time more important than yours.

Instead, command their attention by letting them know how important the next 20 minutes of their life is going to be. Show them why they made the right decision to invest their time with you AND how you're really good at not wasting it. When you meet them, instead of saying, "Thank you for your time" say, "I've got a busy schedule to stick to. Let's jump right in" and start showing them the value. They'll thank you for your time if you do it right.

#5: *You Say You Have an Open Schedule*

Saying something stupid like, "I'm open any time this week, what works well for you?" sounds weak and desperate AF. Producers and players don't have open schedules. You give the prospect an exact time and place. If they are already booked, ask them if they can cancel it. This shows that you're important and confident. If they say they can't cancel, give them another firm alternative.

Since prospects aren't looking at your paychecks and bank account, the only thing they can measure against you is the importance of their time vs. yours. If you sell them on how important your time is, curiosity alone can get you the meeting. People like dealing with people who are busy. Nobody hires the person whose schedule is *wide open*. Being busy plays to the universal law of social proof. If you're busy, that means you're in demand and if you're in demand, you *must* be good.

In the habit of doing one of the above listed actions? *Stop it*! The reason you're not closing as many sales as you want is because your prospect knows you need a sale and they will hold that sale hostage against you. Don't let them see you sweat. I gave you alternative solutions on how to handle each dead giveaway. Now, use what you've learned and go make more sales.

If you're in sales and you're ready to step up your game, whether you're just getting started, or you're scaling a big team, I've got your back. It doesn't matter if you're training yourself or your team. I've got the sales training that will work across the board. Look no further. Grab your access to www.showupandclose.com and start programming yourself for sales success.

If you're ready to invest in your personal success and you'd like to find out about the programs we have developed especially for you, simply head over to www.HardcoreCloser.com/tribe and we'll have a sales conversation about your future.

Chapter 7

Five Free Things You Can Do Right Now to Drum Up Sales

Sometimes, we simply forget to do the things we know to do. We get so busy doing our day-to-day activities that we abandon the actions that got us business and busy in the first place. The thing is, actions create reactions. If you're not taking action, you're not soliciting a reaction.

I'll remind you of some actions you can take to drum up some immediate business no matter how many deals you currently have in your pipeline. I mean, who are we kidding? We can always use more deals in our pipeline. We're in sales. There's never enough.

Here are Five Free Things You Can Do Right Now to Drum Up Sales:

#1: Email Your Existing Prospect List

You have a database of prospects and current clients. When's the last time you emailed them something of value paired with a call to action? I email my lists daily. If you're not staying in front of your audience, they will forget you. We live in the attention economy. Get all you can.

It's your job to remind your audience you're open and available for business. On average, only 15 percent of emails get read, so it's a good idea to email often. At least, send emails out once a week. It costs you nothing to copy and paste a few emails into a message. Warning: don't spam. I'm not suggesting you spam. Make sure you only email people who have given you permission to email.

#2: Call Past Clients and Ask for Referrals

The vast majority of salespeople fail to ask for referrals, mostly because they know they didn't earn the right to ask. For those of us who do earn the right to ask, ask! Prospects don't automatically give you names of people to call and sell your stuff to. You have to earn and ask for referrals.

Call your past clients who were 100 percent satisfied with your services. Ask them how they are enjoying the product. Ask them if they need help or have questions for you. Ask them for referrals. It's real easy to do, so just do it!

#3: Call Clients of Salespeople Who No Longer Work with You

At first, this may feel shady, but if your colleagues no longer work for the company and the company owns the book of business, you'd be a fool not to get your shovel and run into this goldmine. You don't even have to let them know the other guy is gone. Just call and say you're from another department, here to help.

Chances are, most of the prospects bought due to the company and the brand, rather than the actual salesman. Besides, the other guy that quit or got fired…well, they might be gone for a good reason. He or she may also have skipped over a ton of awesome leads who are just waiting to throw their credit cards at you.

#4: Network Through Social Media

The days of driving to a meeting, wasting gas, buying lunch and making small talk for an hour are over. Thanks to social media, you can network with 10 people online in half the time it takes to network with one offline. If you're not spending a portion of your day getting active on pages and in groups, you're missing out on some solid networking opportunities.

Reaching out to people on Facebook and other sites doesn't have to be creepy. Act the exact same way when you're networking on social media as you would if you were to attend a cocktail party or charity function. Be interested, interesting and professional. If you've earned the right to do so, ask for the business. But only do this if you've provided enough value to ask. Treat online business

EXACTLY like offline.

#5: *Reach Out to Referral Sources*

When I sold cars and it was slow, I'd cold call insurance agents to see how I could help people making claims on crashed cars. I reached out to the top 100 insurance agencies and spoke to many agents. I'd offer to train them on social media marketing in exchange for sending me people who had totaled cars. Insurance agents were excellent sources of referrals for me.

What referral sources are you not chasing? There are plenty of people in your market who need your services. There are plenty of other people who sell to those people. Find them. Close them. Get referrals from them.

If you're looking for someone to help remind you of what you need to be doing, as well as arm you with the best ways to attract perfect customers and close easy sales, I'd suggest you look at www.inboundleadcloser.com and buy it. My program will turn you into a lead-generating, sales-closing machine through repetition.

If you're ready to invest in your personal success and you'd like to find out about the programs we have developed especially for you, simply head over to www.HardcoreCloser.com/tribe and we'll have a sales conversation about your future.

Chapter 8

Why People Buy BS vs. the Real Thing

The world is full of bullshitters. Game recognizes game and BS recognizes BS. Everyone is searching for the lazy way to get rich, make sales and all that fun stuff. Just two generations ago, we preached about hard work. In present day, we preach people should work smarter, not harder. This paradigm shift has screwed up a lot of people's thinking. People believe they are smart AND they are working, so that must mean they are working smart. The truth is most people aren't anywhere near as smart as they think they are. I have a lot of idiots tell me how intelligent they are.

Now that we've established that people aren't working as "smart" as they think, let's get deeper. What if most people work dumb? Knowing what to do and doing it are two different stories. Everyone knows you need to market, advertise and sell to get paid. Yet, many of us will go days at a time without taking the necessary action to make a big paycheck. Working smart doesn't mean being lazy. Just because you are smart doesn't mean you shouldn't work hard. Why not do both? I know why!

When someone's selling a "push button, get-rich-the-lazy-way" product vs. your "real deal, let's-get-to-work" product, they will take the lazy way nine times out of ten. Why? Because if they fail on the "get-rich-the-lazy-way" program they can blame the program. But if they fail at the "real deal, hard work" program, they have to take personal responsibility. People hate owning up to their own shit. They will do anything to blame anyone but themselves for their circumstances.

If what you sell is real, then it naturally requires some action in order to make it work. People run from real work. Everyone wants to get rich and be like Warren Buffet, but no one is willing to do the work he's done. We live in a time when overnight celebrities are sensationalized. Everyone is just sitting around, in permanent purgatory, waiting for someone to see them and make them rich.

Newsflash: it doesn't work that way. Just because you see it every day, doesn't mean it happens. There's only about one or two viral videos each month, which equates to about 150 overnight successes a year. Out of seven billion people, what makes you think you're going to be one of the one-fifty? You're better off playing the lotto. Plus, those same viral videos and overnight celebrities put in the work. What you don't see is the work. Why? Work is not cool or glorious, so no one talks about it. Everyone wants a trophy, but not everyone is willing to practice and play.

Now back to the BS vs. real thing. The world is full of prospects just waiting on their shot, praying that one day someone will see them and *give* it to them. As someone who was seen and given a shot, I can tell you the shot I got was because the person who offered it saw me working my ass off.

Jordan Belfort is a prime example. He got rich promising people they could get rich the lazy way. Meanwhile the legit stockbrokers on Wall Street selling legit products made nowhere near what he did.

Here's how you fix it:

Be present, be real and be confrontational with the thinking of your prospects. Show them if the "push button, get-rich-the-lazy-way" worked, we'd all be rich and lazy, yet here we are, still doing life like we always do. Take their delusions of grandeur and push them back to reality. Do it from a place of love and respect and they will see you actually care and have the real deal. If that doesn't work, they deserve to have their money taken. Just remember to charge them double when they come back to you complaining later.

If you make over $25,000 in gross commissions each month, I'd like to speak with you about how I can help you get to $100,000.

If you're ready to invest in your personal success and you'd like to find out about the programs we have developed especially for you, simply head over to www.HardcoreCloser.com/tribe and we'll have a sales conversation about your future.

Chapter 9

Taking the COLD Out of Cold Calling

These days, most people don't realize cold calling is one of the least effective ways to make a sale. It's annoying to the salesman, it's an inefficient waste of time and prospects hate it. Those three things alone should be enough to cut out cold calls permanently. For a lot of you, it's not.

Every time, I talk about how I hate cold calls, there's always one salesman who says, "It's different in my business," or "You're just not good at them." I've made more cold calls than I want to admit. I've made so many I decided six years ago I'd never make another one. I got sick and tired of wasting my time trying to talk to people who didn't want to talk to me.

Eliminating cold calls is a bold move for a salesman to make. Much like many of you reading this, I relied on cold calls to make sales. It wasn't 100 percent of my business, but in 2010, cold calling brought in a lot of deals for me. For every sale it brought in, there were 50 unanswered calls, 30 hang-ups, 10 disconnected numbers and nine people talking to me who would rather have watched paint dry.

Face it, the only reason you make cold calls is because your outdated, no-selling, cheap-ass sales manager requires it. He knows if you make 300 calls a day, you'll make 1-2 sales daily. It's what he did, so it's all he knows. When he sold whatever it is you're cold calling about now, there were no social media, email or any of the other tools you can use to contact people. He's old school and now he's forcing you to go old school, too.

There's a Better Way to Make Money Than Cold Calling.

If you could make 1-2 sales each day in 10 calls instead of 300, your sales manager might actually show an interest in what you are doing. Instead, you're stuck making calls all day which leaves you with no time to try experiments on your own. Don't worry, I've got you! I'll show you how to take the "cold" out of cold calling.

There's a big difference in how a conversation takes place with a stranger vs. how it goes down with someone you know. Even if you've only heard of a person, you're more likely to speak with them on the phone than you would a complete stranger. I've got a method you'll love! Let me help you out.

First, you've got to get clear on who it is you can help. Instead of machine gunning cold calls, we are going to take sniper shots at sure things. Yes, it's a different battle plan than you are used to, but trust me it's a lot more effective and lucrative. Get clear on who you want to work with by making a list of 50-100 perfect prospects. The perfect prospect is someone who you know would benefit from what you sell and would be a dream client to have. I'm talking name, email, address and phone number for everyone on the list. Learn to use Google.

Instead of machine gunning cold calls let me show you the sniper sales strategy. Take the time you would normally use to blast out cold calls to actually do some social reconnaissance and find out a little about your prospect. The main thing you are looking for is what sports teams they post about, what college they went to, who their idols are and what type of books they likely read.

Once you know what the prospect is into, your next step is to get what they like to them. What I do is go to Amazon and order books they would read. You can get a used book for $4 or so. Since you have their name, email and address, you can send the book directly from Amazon. You can even have Amazon put a note in the book for no extra charge. Make the note say something like this:

"John,

I admire your work and the corporation you've built. You remind me of Elon Musk. Have you heard of him? He's changing the way the world does business, just like you. I thought you'd really enjoy this biography and you could possibly use it as inspiration to do even more for the business world than what you have already accomplished.

I'll be reaching out to you in a few days to make sure you received this book. I know you'll love it and I want to make sure it was delivered to the right hands. I'll be calling from 214-555-6565 so you'll know it's me. Talk with you soon – Ryan"

A quick, off-the-cuff note paired with a book you know they will love to read, will change the conversation from "Buy my stuff, I'm a cold caller," to "I'm the guy who sent you a gift, just making sure you got it." All you're trying to do as a salesman is get the attention of your best and most potentially profitable audience.

In a world full of selfish salesmen, a gift-giver stands out. This doesn't only work for books either. One time, I got a card in the mail from Kent Clothier that had a little TV on it with a video inviting me to an event. As busy as I was, and as packed as my schedule was, I, and several other high-level guys made the trek to meet Kent. His video card was the contact method that sealed the deal. Use your imagination and stay within your budget.

You might already be thinking "I don't have money

to send books," but come on, get real. A cup of coffee at Starbucks is seven bucks. You can get a used book for four. If you make 300 cold calls each day and send out three books to the top three prospects, you'll most likely make the same amount of sales using less time and effort because you simply sent the value first.

We live in a time where you have to stand out to make a sale. Cold calling insinuates *what can you do for me?* Gift giving tips the scales on the law of reciprocity. Your recipients will almost feel like they owe you a phone call because you went the extra mile (where others won't go.)

Save yourself some time, slow down on cold calling and get better at social recon and gift giving. You'll stand out above all the rest. I've also found that most times the prospect will call me. That's why I leave my number on the note. Don't knock it until you try it.

Ready to step into the new age way of selling? Just order www.buyshowupandclose.com. FULL of stealthy tactics like the one in this blog post, you'll learn making money means acting like you're a sniper, not a machine gunner. Show Up and Close turns you into a sniper.

If you're ready to invest in your personal success and you'd like to find out about the programs we

have developed especially for you, simply head over to www.HardcoreCloser.com/tribe and we'll have a sales conversation about your future.

Chapter 10

How to Close Sales Without Ever Picking Up the Phone

"You used to call me on my cell phone..." Never mind being mad at me for getting Drake stuck in your head (again), this chapter reminded me of that song. And if it's going to be stuck in my head while I'm writing it, it's going to get stuck in yours while you read it.

People don't really use the phone that much anymore. There. I said it. I know 90 percent of you are calling me an idiot and saying this is not true. I'm not saying the phone is dead and you can't make money from it. I'm just saying it's on life support and if you don't have the vision to see it, you need glasses.

According to a study conducted by AT&T in 2012, 2011 was the last year we talked. They reported 86 percent of all calls went unanswered and we text and email more than we talk. The numbers don't lie. If only 14 percent of your calls get answered and people are avoiding the phone more and more, why fight it? This was in 2012, so I'm sure the percentages have increased.

I'm an early adopter, and I've watched this trend

since 2012. I'm not going to be the guy who goes broke and says, "I never saw it coming." If I'd have owned a Blockbuster store when Netflix came on the scene, I'd have closed shop real quick and bought a Redbox. Sadly, many folks wait until the last minute to embrace something new.

The Way We Communicate is Changing

Here's an eye opener. All the new apps that come out, all the new social media sites that come out, none of them are based on the telephone. They are all designed to be used with text and video. People are evolving away from the phone. If you've read Napoleon Hill's *Think and Grow Rich* book, you know he talks about the future and communicating with microwaves. We are here, but those microwaves are smart phones.

When you think of aliens, you don't think of them picking up phones and talking. You picture them communicating via mind reading or something like that. Ray Kurzweil says in the year 2030, we will have chips embedded in our brain to help us process data. I believe that's when the phone will become a part of us. With Google Glass, it's already happening.

Technology is Making Great Strides to Get Rid of the Phone Completely

Do I think we will wake up tomorrow and phones will be gone? No. I do think that by 2030, they will be a memory. How many times each day does your phone ring, and it's someone you like, but you still don't answer? Think about how many times that happens to other people each day, too. Folks, it's painfully obvious people are dodging the phone.

Now look, I'm just like you. I'm a BAMF on the phone. I love the phone. I live and die by it still, but only as a last resort. The only time I get on the phone with someone is when they ask me to. If someone hits me up via email, I keep the conversation there. I'm not going to sell them on getting on the phone with me when I can sell them on buying my shit via email.

How Many of Your Clients Prefer to Only Communicate Via Email or Text?

Right now, I'm sure you have several people who've asked you to communicate with them via text or email only. This is not the wave of the future. It's the present time, my friend. You'd do best to expect that everyone under the age of 60 prefers to communicate via text of some sort.

It's easier to close someone where they are comfortable already, than to try and get them out of their comfort zone. When prospects get pulled out of their comfort zone, they get scared and anxious.

The last thing you want is a prospect with anxiety towards you, even the tiniest little bit. It's much simpler to keep the conversation flowing where your prospect feels comfortable communicating.

How to Close Sales Without Ever Picking Up the Phone

First, you need to become proficient at typing and texting. Saying: "Aw man, I suck at typing!" is a pathetic excuse. I took typing one semester in the 7th grade and I've been okay at it ever since. It's not that you suck at it; it's that you are too lazy to man up and master a new form of communication. *That stung didn't it?*

A master salesman can sell anything from anywhere. I sell from text, email, video, blog posts, in person, on stage, in the air, on land and over social media. I've adapted to every communication platform there is and I highly suggest you do the same. If you choose not to, you will eventually be left behind. Look around the office, see that gray-haired dude who's old, broke and should have retired 10 years ago? Yeah, that's your future if you don't adopt and take heed to my warning.

You should be able to text and type in a way that sounds exactly like how you talk. It's not about being formal or having perfect punctuation. It's about being able to effectively and quickly communicate with your fingers. It's like learning another language, but way easier. Bring the conversation to your prospects with text and they will be more apt to buy from you. I sold a $20,000 membership last night, via text on a Facebook chat. True story.

Here's how to become a better writer and make your sales writing skills match your vocal game. Go to Amazon and buy books on copywriting—not like patents and copyrighting—copywriting: how to write persuasively. There are a ton of resources out there. Matter of fact, that's how I learned to write blog posts. At some point, my typing matched up with my speaking.

Practice.

I've got a program and process that focuses on closing prospects on other communication mediums besides the phone. I'm not saying avoid the phone, I'm just saying you can score more sales by mastering all types of communication, too. Even in high-end B2B text and email platforms. Check out www.inboundleadcloser.com for all the details.

If you're ready to invest in your personal success and you'd like to find out about the programs we have developed especially for you, simply head over to www.HardcoreCloser.com/tribe and we'll have a sales conversation about your future.

Chapter 11

How to Overcome the "Do You Have Any Success Stories?" Objection When You're New in Sales

When you are first getting started off in any sales business, it's hard. There. I said it. I wasn't kidding either. Seems like every time I've ever started a new business the prospects must have had "new" radar. And when prospects spot a green pea, they almost always throw out the one objection that's hard as hell to counter without sounding like a total idiot douche. You've heard it. I've heard it. And we have both looked like morons when they hit us with it.

"Do you have any people who I can call and ask for testimonials?"

It's as if they know you don't, and they are trying to win some sort of *I'm Right* contest. Meanwhile, you've been talking to them, showing off your product like you've been in the business 25+ years. So, then you have to explain why you know so much, but have sold so little.

It sucks. It's embarrassing and it happens to all of us. Being a pro salesman is all about adaptation, though. You've got to set the proper expectations up front. When you're new, don't pretend to be anything other than what you are.

When I started selling cars, people would come in and ask me questions about horsepower, etc. Now, I'm not a car guy. I can't change a tire or oil and I don't know anything mechanical. I also gave my bud, Sal $100 to take the car tests for me, so I could get certified. Literally, I didn't know shit.

When I had questions I didn't know the answers to, I'd just tell the prospects, "I don't know, but I will find out for you before we close the deal." This allowed my prospects to see firsthand I wasn't a know-it-all salesman. It also showed them I was resourceful and able to get the information they needed.

Meanwhile, when you're in the consulting business, it's different. We sell success, and people want to see others who have bought and obtained that success from us. When you're new, you obviously don't have the track record to show anyone your list of happy clients. So, what do you do?

When I had my first conversation with Steve Green, he told me he was in a spot. He said his top agent had just left the business and he needed to replace her ASAP. I told him what I could do and showed him how easily we could put it into play.

When Steve asked me what people he could talk to

about my stuff, I was straight up with him and said, "I don't have any. So far, I'm the first and only person to do this stuff. It worked for me. It will work for you. When it's all said and done I want YOU to be the guy people call to get testimonials about my work. You'll be that guy, but it starts with a decision to work with me now."

I didn't have to lie. I didn't send him to a fake testimonial person. None of that was needed. He just needed the reassurance I was going to do what I said. And of course I did exactly that. Now, Steve has been a client for over two years. When someone reaches out to me who needs to hear a third party, I send them to Steve.

He now does exactly what I told him he would do on that first phone call. I promised to make him the guy, and I did.

As salesmen, we are tempted to cut corners because we know our prospects usually don't trust our word. I've done my 100 percent best to live by my word and I still get static. I can imagine what the "average guy" goes through.

So, instead of trying to BS your way into your first client, just be up front, set expectations and tell them you want to make THEM the first and best testimonial you'll ever have. There's a catch to this, though. It's not just sunshine and rainbows when you make this promise to them.

YOU HAVE TO FOLLOW THROUGH!!!

Once you tell them they're your number one, your next job is to serve them like you'll never have another client. Since you don't have a lot of clients, you can take the time to make their experience the best. You CAN follow up with them to ensure everything is working according to plan.

If they take a chance on you, knowing you're a rookie, you'd better go above and beyond to make a friggin' example out of them. Do 10x whatever it is they expect. When you do this, they will also be more than happy to provide future testimonies for you. But only if you make an example out of 'em.

If you're ready to invest in your personal success and you'd like to find out about the programs we have developed especially for you, simply head over to www.HardcoreCloser.com/tribe and we'll have a sales conversation about your future.

Chapter 12

How to Handle the Price Objection and Close Over It Like a Boss

It's one thing to encounter a cheapskate, but most times it's the salesman's fault to begin with. In my Facebook group, Sales Talk with Sales Pros, members often ask, "How do I handle the price objection?" Price is something we all struggle with. The price is the final step in getting an agreement leading in to the close.

Let's face it, most of us don't slap the lowest price tag on what we sell or provide. I don't think I've ever worked for the "cheapest place" in my past. I wouldn't, and didn't want to. Cheap places attract cheapskates. That being said, you can't close on price alone, unless you are, in fact, the cheapest. The public knows you get what you pay for, though. So, don't discount this fact.

The problem with cheapskates is they've been programmed this way. Oftentimes, through your own marketing. For example, if you sell mortgages and you state: "We have the lowest rates," you can't get upset when you get rate shopped. Same goes for cars; you can't say you're the cheapest, then get mad when your prospect double checks to make sure you're right.

If you're talking and negotiating on price, you screwed the sales process up. Don't worry; if you're currently doing this, I'm going to teach you how to knock it off.

Your ONLY goal as a salesperson should be to move the prospect from reality to their desired outcome. If you help them reach their desired outcome, you'll earn your desired income. Once you've done this properly, price won't be an issue.

Think about it. Kohl's and Nordstrom both sell black pants. Nordstrom's pants are five times the price. People go in to Nordstrom's and feel good about buying overpriced pants. Shoppers at Kohl's, where they offer a percentage off everything, will use Kohl's Cash and discounts to negotiate their price as low as possible. No one negotiates at Nordstrom. Nordstrom's rarely even holds sales.

There are certain steps you have to take, in order to effectively avoid the price objection. No salesman likes to get to the end of the selling process then have to start over again, this time selling price instead of the product. I like to be efficient, and making two sales on one person isn't the best use of my time, unless one of those sales is an upsell.

Here's What You Do Instead: ASK QUESTIONS!

It's your job to be a detective. You need to be on the

lookout for buying clues, so that you can solve the sales mystery. You never see an episode of *CSI* where they talk the suspect into confessing. Instead, what they do is ask him questions *until* he confesses. Take note, that's how sales works, too.

How can you sell the prospect something, if you don't know what they want? Most likely, the prospect doesn't want what you sell, they want the outcome what you sell provides. In other words, no one wants a drill; they want a hole. No one wants a mortgage; they want a house. What is it you're really selling? It's an *outcome*, not a product.

As soon as you make the shift from selling products to selling outcomes, you'll see your closing ratio increase significantly. As a salesperson, the less you talk, the more you make. We salesmen hate dead silence. We think it's our job to fill that dead air. It is. But it's meant to be filled by the prospect, not the salesman. Ask questions. Let the prospect answer and look for buying clues.

What if the prospect hits you with, "So what's this gonna cost me?" right out of the gate. It's simple. You break the frame and control the prospect by replying, "We'll determine that based on what it is that you want and need. So, tell me what made you decide to reach out to us?" Start the questions right then. They will have a hard time resisting answering the questions.

While asking them questions, you're looking for desired outcomes. Once you have a keen idea of what it is they want from using your products, that's when you start *stacking the value*. I'm still not talking price either. Let's say you're selling a sports car to a 50+-year old single dude and you find out he's really into handjobs from twenty-somethings. Before talking price, talk about how this car is a chick magnet, and the young ones love it, etc.

Stack the Value, Then Talk Price

If you've uncovered the desired outcome, stacked the value and price is STILL a f'n problem, you most likely missed a crucial clue. Start the questioning process again to find out what you missed. Like I said in the beginning, some people are just cheapskates, but when you follow this process, you'll be able to bump off a lot of cheapskates, too.

If you've been in sales for any period of time, you've run into cheaple (cheap people) and you've lost deals over price. No matter your skill level, my sales program will help you increase your closing ratios, and decrease your TDs. Check out my online sales training program Show Up and Close. Give me space in your head for 60 days and I'll change your life.

If you're ready to invest in your personal success

and you'd like to find out about the programs we have developed especially for you, simply head over to www.HardcoreCloser.com/tribe and we'll have a sales conversation about your future.

Chapter 13

How to Relentlessly Close Over Objections Without Pissing Off Prospects

First off, before we even get too far into this, can we just both agree that objections are bullshit excuses people use to avoid making a decision? People run from making decisions, especially hard ones. Decisions come with consequences. Most people have made a ton of bad decisions and have linked negative consequences to the decisions they've made.

Yeah, I know. I went pretty deep on you right there. In order to get where I need you to go in this one, I had to go there quick. Damn, I tried to edit that previous sentence, but, confusing as it is, it's the only way I can get it to make sense.

To Relentlessly Close Over Objections, You Must Establish Control First.

The sale starts the second the prospect sees you or your advertisement. The first glance at your product or brand is the beginning point of the sell. It's at that same first glance, that the prospect decides if you are some sort of expert or authority on what it is you sell. You've got to gain the prospect's respect from the jump.

Closing is not one big ideal of a sale. Closing is the finishing point of a series of sales being made. For example, when a prospect sees your ad and decides to take you up on the call to action, that's a sale. You sold them on taking action. From there, when the prospect enters their information, that's another sale. And so on and so on…

It's ONLY After You've Made All the Little Sales, That You Can Close the One Sale That Gets You Paid

Now, with all of that background information out of the way, let's talk about relentlessly closing over objections. Relentless, in this case, means to press on as if the objections have not even been given. It means to completely ignore the objection in its context and accept it for what it is: an "excuse" not to make a decision.

Once you operate with this mindset, you'll be able to treat objections how they need to be treated. Like a little bitch! Just know that objections are coming. You've got to do your best as a master sales artist, to overcome as many as you can BEFORE they come up. When you're in the presentation or demo part of the sale, use it to address the common objections for the prospect and overcome them all at once.

Each one of the little sales steps will come with an

objection. Identifying these objections is key to overcoming them. Too many salespeople operate reactively when it comes to sales objections. A master salesman knows to be proactive with objections and handle as many as he can BEFORE he asks for the business.

Proactively Addressing and Handling Objections Separates the Order Takers from the Closers

Most sales people treat objections like curve balls. They act like they've never seen one thrown before, even though they are thrown in damn near every at bat attempt. You shouldn't be surprised or afraid of objections. You need to know they exist, why they exist and what prompts them to come up. Once you make yourself aware, you can easily be on alert for when they are about to make an appearance.

I'd encourage you to take a few minutes to make a list of the usual objections that come up in your business. There's at least 20 of them, so don't short yourself. Everything from "I can't afford it" to "I need to ask my wife" should be on that list. After you've gotten your 20 or so objections down, write under each one the reason why this objection comes up. Then under that, write why that objection is bullshit. And under that, you write down how to overcome it.

Making a List of Common Objections and Solutions Empowers You as a Sales Closer

When you're proactive and handling objections up front, you are taking power away from your prospect. Then the usual bullshit, go-to excuses they plan on using are taken away from them. If this were a fighting video game their power bar would be decreasing and the announcer would be about to say "*FINISH HIM!* "

When you look at sales as a series of small sales with small objections that lead to a close, you gain much more power and authority over the prospect. They become defenseless. When there's nothing else to say but "I'll take it," or "Take my money," you've done your job. Handling sales objections using my process keeps the tension down, too.

Closing Over Objections Up Front Prevents Prospects from Getting Emotional or Angry

Often, a salesperson will get into a battle of egos with the prospect, and will wait until the close to try and dominate. More times than not, it's too late at this point. If you haven't closed your small sales, you won't close the big one. Especially if your ego allows you to say something that pisses off the prospect.

The last thing you want is to get to the close, piss

the prospect off and then have to make another sale. Then you'll have to sell to get them back to liking you and work even harder once more to get back to the close. The easiest way to do this is to simply close them up front. Each little sale is a trial close. Get them used to being closed and they WILL close.

Speaking of closing, if you want to know more about how I close sales, how my process works and how you can use tactics like this to make a fortune selling whatever it is you want to sell, check out my fail proof program www.showupandclose.com. I promise if you invest, take action and do what I teach, your income will drastically increase.

If you're ready to invest in your personal success and you'd like to find out about the programs we have developed especially for you, simply head over to www.HardcoreCloser.com/tribe and we'll have a sales conversation about your future.

Chapter 14

How to Use Technology to Build, Train, and Grow an Elite Sales Team Without Investing a Lot of Your Time and Resources

It never fails. Every day I get at least one message or email from someone who asks me if I know a good salesperson who needs a job. I send the exact same reply to all of them. "If I knew a good salesman who wanted a job, I'd hire him." I'm dead serious. Good salespeople are hard to find. Here's why—someone is paying them what they are worth.

Lots of People Think They're Good at Sales, Truth is, Your Paycheck Determines That.

Sales are about one thing and one thing only: making money. None of us are in this game for the thrill of it. We deal with turndowns, hang ups and slammed doors every day in order to get paid— nothing more, nothing less. Those of us who have found our way are almost always un-hirable.

That being said, most of us have to settle with hiring someone who's more "okay" at sales than "good." Then it's our job to train them into being a "good" salesman, which after years and decades of doing, can be exhausting. Especially since most of us train people who then go on to become a competitor in one form or another.

For the last five years, I've run a lifestyle business that didn't require a sales team, but late last year, I realized I was being selfish and playing small. I had hired and trained mortgage teams before, but honestly, it was a pain in my ass. I've got the patience of a toddler and the mouth of someone with Tourette's, so I usually just fire people and do it myself.

I had an incident in my life where an attorney had to evaluate my business. When he got back to me, he told me it was not a business, it was just me hustling and if I got sick, hurt, or killed…then the business was worthless. He suggested I create a sales force to push my digital products. As much as I didn't want to hire and train a sales force, I knew I was going to have to.

I Got to Work on Recruiting and Training a Sales Team

Last fall, I started hiring sales people. I put the word on the street I was looking for good salespeople and all sorts of folks showed up. Hungry, ready, eager to make big money. Sadly, none of the original line-up is even around now, which is just a few months later as I write this. I hired and fired around 10 salespeople in a very short period of time. Within that same time frame, I also found a solid crew who seems to be performing happily and growing my business with me.

I created this team with minimal amounts of my time invested. As an entrepreneur with multiple businesses to run and hundreds of clients to help, I have to make sure to use my time in the absolute best way possible. What I did allowed me to not only train a group who's closing around $40,000 in commissioned sales each month, I also spend less than two hours a week training and helping them.

I use a conference call service and I have my sales team call in every Monday, Wednesday and Friday at 9am Texas time. The calls are usually 5-20 minutes long and they serve two purposes. Purpose one is to micro-train salespeople in small segments to avoid overwhelm. Purpose two is to keep my crew motivated. Motivation expires quickly, so I bring the heat three days each week.

I Lead the Team from the Front Lines, as I Make Calls and Close Sales

By leading the team from the front lines, they see what can be done and aspire to do the same. I'm not some lame duck manager, who hasn't closed a sale in years, yelling at my crew about why they can't close shit. I'm out here, showing them how it's done on a daily basis. The team knows I wouldn't ask them to do anything I'm not already doing myself.

I use these conference calls to talk about my vision, what I'm personally doing that works and to drill the same word tracks into their heads over and over again. I also use these calls to constantly up the pace. I'm all about growing and expanding, so I make sure I keep that vision congruent with my team, too. I want them to do more, close more and have more each and every month. There is no point where we believe "We made it!" because we always want more.

Another key component to being able to train my team without taking up all my time has been to record everything. I've recorded every sales training call, every webinar I've ever done and every question I've been asked. I have a FAQ type of page that contains everything my team needs. Before they come to me, they know to go to that program page and get the info.

They Buy and Implement My Show Up and Close Sales Training Program

Also, I require each of my salespeople to buy my Show Up and Close program and implement what they learn. This way, they are selling the exact same thing they've already bought, and believe in. They also know exactly what the client will be getting, the process and all. This makes them a question and objection-handling animal after about 60 days.

Here's a blatant but worthy sales pitch:

If you're a business owner or manager, you should purchase my sales training programs for your sales staff. This keeps you from having to train them too extensively. They learn your products and services, and when they use my word tracks, they won't be asking YOU questions, they'll be asking the prospects questions, like a good salesperson's supposed to do. If you want to increase your sales exponentially, get your team's hands on my program at www.buyshowupandclose.com.

My team also uses a group chat I created and at this point they all answer each other's questions. They self-rely on the FAQ page or chat BEFORE they reach out to me. I've set the expectation for them to respect my time. They will ask each other via the group chat before they hit me or my operations manager up. A majority of the time, one person on the team will know the answer and help.

Training a good sales team doesn't have to take all your time and energy. I think it all starts with getting clear on who can stay around. I've given chances to a lot of people to be on the team, yet I make cuts like a pro ball team in pre-season. Anyone can talk the talk, but I only need to see a few steps to see how they walk. Using cheap and free technology will save you time and money to accomplish other, more meaningful tasks.

If you're ready to invest in your personal success and you'd like to find out about the programs we have developed especially for you, simply head over to www.HardcoreCloser.com/tribe and we'll have a sales conversation about your future.

Chapter 15

Why Settling for a Six-figure Income in Sales is a Bad Idea

I'm gonna just come out and say it. "Being a millionaire is the new middle class." *There.* In my parent's day, making $100K/year meant something. In today's times, making $100K in 12 months can leave you completely broke. Half goes to taxes and if you pay $2,000/month in rent, 75 percent of your income is gone from the jump. That leaves you with only $25,000 to pay all your bills for the year.

Earning a Six-figure Income in Sales Isn't All It's Cracked Up to Be

You may be reading this right now, making $70,000/year and wondering what in the hell I'm talking about. Sure, six figures can change things for a lot of people, but let's face it, when you make more money, all you do is spend more money. Don't act like you're different. You're in sales. You get the bug to blow cash just like the rest of us.

The key is to outearn your spending habits. Trust me, at $100,000 or so annual income, you'll wind up at the end of the year with nothing. Why you ask? Because psychologically you've been taught your whole life that earning six figures is being rich and most of us blow our cash accordingly.

Worse yet, most of us salesmen suffer from an upper limit problem. If we think we have too much money saved up, we either get lazy at work or we spend it. Nothing is going to change for you at $100K that wasn't already happening for you at $70K. You'll only find a way to blow even more money.

In many cases, salesmen end up doing dumb shit with the extra income they make. They buy drugs, bottle service and fancier cars than they have driven in the past. These three items are a 100 percent waste of your money if you're only earning a lower six-figure income annually.

If You're Not Saving Money Earning $75,000 a Year, You Won't Save Money Earning $100,000.

Sure, I know you're sitting there, reading this, thinking *I'm different. I'll pay off my bills, give to charity*, etc. It's all bullshit. You tell yourself these things, but money changes people. We ALWAYS find a way to spend what we got. You can deny it all you want, but as a guy who earns it and who has helped countless others earn it, I'm just telling you from firsthand experience.

Enough doom and gloom over having first world income earning problems. Let's talk about what goals to set and how to achieve them. I'm not here to knock your income, I'm here to show you why and how you can be doing more. Doesn't matter what income level you are at now; you can do what I'm about to teach you.

The first thing you have to do, and this is a must, is get your thinking up. If you think $100,000 is a lot of money, you are mistaken. By letting a six-figure income intimidate you, you're only guaranteeing that you will screw it up once you get there. Or worse yet, settle for it.

If you've spent your whole life imagining what it's like to earn $100,000 in a year, and then you get there, you'll settle and think that's where you want to stay forever. Consider this instead: once you get your goals up and aimed toward earning seven figures, you'll see an increase in your thinking. Start looking at a million dollars the same way you looked at one hundred thousand.

When you look at a hundred grand, you think it's attainable and you see a path to get there. Yet, deep in the back of your mind you want a million. The million just seems too far off to attain. Guess what? It's not. It just takes some increase in thought waves and a decrease in respect for the money game.

Earning a Seven-figure Income in Sales is Not as Hard as it Seems!

You may sell cars, real estate, or mortgages and think *I work my ass off to make a six-figure income in sales. It's impossible to earn seven figures in twelve months at what I do.* That's okay, but I'm going to show you where you are wrong. You need more than one stream of income. You need more than two.

The goal of three income sources is to produce a minimum of six figures in annual income *in each stream.* Having three sources of income, each producing a minimum of $100K annually, is no longer a six-figure income, it's a multiple six-figure income. You can bankroll a multiple six-figure annual income into seven figures a lot easier than you think.

Let's say you sell real estate. In order to make $100,000 annually as an agent, you need to sell roughly 17 homes at $200,000 each, collecting three percent commission. The average agent, by the way, sells only three homes each year. What I'm saying is 17 homes is way above average for agents. Most agents think $100,000 is about all the money they can make unless they sell higher value homes.

The key is to simply add another bolt onto the service you already sell. As an agent, you should also buy, sell and rent your personal real estate. Let's say you flip four homes each year. Every 90 days you should be buying, rehabbing and selling a home. Each flip is going to net you at least $25,000 cash, unless you're buying ultra-cheap properties (this involves the bank giving out loans or hard money—so, I don't recommend it.)

You're already selling homes. Why not take on a minimum of four safe projects each year? Most people don't do it because they are lazy. They don't want to put in the additional work. Most people try to earn an additional income in a totally unrelated field. That's not wise.

Look for Ways to Earn Additional Streams of Incomes to Complement Your Main Income

Keeping with the same example. but using a real estate agent instead, you could also bird-dog properties for other investors. Simply find 10 homes each year with a $5,000 margin, so you can make a birddog fee. It isn't that hard. It's actually less than one property location and securement each month.

Even better, you could be like me and teach others how to get leads and close deals; you could tell them all about your process for extra money. It's called "consulting" and if you're making $100,000 a year, you can surely help someone who's making $75,000 get there. People usually pay $5,000 per person which means you only need 20 clients annually to earn another $100,000 doing what you already do.

For those of you in the car biz, you can flip cars easier than agents flip houses. You've got no excuses either. If you're a full-time consultant now, find ways to affiliate market other products as well as to create your own. There's no reason to have only one six-figure stream of income when it's too easy to have multiple streams.

Lastly, you grow each of these businesses annually, bankroll invest into scaling them and in 3–5 years you could earn an annual income of over seven figures. Guess what? It's gonna take work, though. Just so we are clear, the reason most people don't earn a million is because they refuse to work for it. You gotta do the work! A million bucks isn't just going to hand itself to you.

If you'd like to know how to create additional streams of income that complement your current business, take a look at my latest program www.competitiondemolition.co. It will show you how to craft offers, find niches and advertise your new business to those niches. It's the best program you'll ever invest in.

If you're ready to invest in your personal success and you'd like to find out about the programs we have developed especially for you, simply head over to www.HardcoreCloser.com/tribe and we'll have a sales conversation about your future.

Chapter 16

How to Earn a Million Dollars Per Year in Sales, No Matter What You Sell

A million bucks ain't what it used to be, but it's still a lot. Less than a million people worldwide, make a million or more USD in a 12-month period. It's every person's dream to make a million bucks and be a millionaire. Reaching the seven-figure pinnacle is a fantasy come true for all of us.

Why Do So Many Salesmen Settle for Less Than a Million Dollars Per Year?

First off, making a million bucks in annual income ain't no joke. It takes hard work and in 99 percent of the cases, it takes years of behind the scenes work, too. Most people simply give up! They experience how much work is involved, and they settle. Humans love comfort zones and there's no self-made millionaire who's earned a dime in their comfort zone.

Second off, the people around you will dictate your income. Did you know a goldfish only grows to the size of its surroundings? If you keep it in a tiny bowl it will stay small; if you turn it loose in a pond it will grow as large as it wants. Your circle of influence is the same. If all your friends and coworkers tell you making a million is impossible, you'll believe it and only grow to your surroundings, just like that goldfish.

The people you surround yourself with on a regular basis have the most space in your head. They can stunt your growth and stall your big thinking. I'm telling you this because I know what I'm about to hear from you…

The excuse:
But Ryan, I can't make a million dollars a year at what I do!

Save that BS for someone who'll give you empathy. You won't find that here. Whatever you think, you're right. Wouldn't you rather think big and be right than little and be wrong? You can't say it's impossible for you to earn a million. There are people in your industry doing it, right now. Yes, *your* industry.

Back in the day, people used to say it was impossible to run a 4-minute mile. Now people crush that all day, every day like it's normal. All we needed was social proof that something could be done, and once we received it, others followed suit. Look at the Olympics, records are broken each year. In your industry there are already people making millions, so you know it can be done. You just need to work out hard enough to break those records, too.

The Negativity and Excuses Are Out Into the Light. Let's Talk Money.

Some simple math. $1,000,000/365 days in a year = $2,739.72 every 24 hours. That means you need to earn $114 every hour of the day, 365 days each year. Now let's scale this. How many sales does it take for you to get to $2,739.72? If you sell cars and your average payout is $400/sale, you need to make seven car deals every day you work.

If you're a loan officer, this means you need to close roughly one deal every day. For realtors, this means one deal every three days. For insurance agents, it's about two homeowner's policies per day. It's not as much as you think. It's just a matter of breaking the math down and getting clear about hitting goals.

To most, a million dollars is simply a grandiose number that they dream of. They fantasize about it and talk about it, but most have never even taken the time to do the above math—as simple as it was. Those who have earned a million, have done the math, gotten clear about the numbers and focused on hitting them.

Now you may say, "Ryan, you can't sell seven cars in one day. The most you can sell is three, and that's a lot." Again, I say, "Bullshit." The dealer that owns the place where you work, sells seven…even twenty in a day. Sell seven per day long enough and you'll own the place. You've got to quit thinking small.

You can leverage a team of people to hit your goal, too. Sometimes it's better to make a little off a lot of people than a lot from self-sustaining efforts. If you have a team in place, simply scale your goal accordingly and hit the goal. Making a million dollars in 12 months doesn't have to be complicated or hard.

It's as simple as setting a goal, getting clear on the outcome and working to make it happen.

The first step toward making a million a year is to map out the plan. What are you gonna sell, how many do you need to sell and what kind of help do you need to hit those numbers? Once you get that math down, DO NOT relent until you've achieved what you want. Trust me; the second million is way easier.

The key to earning a million is to work for it. You can't quit if you don't get it in year one, two, or three. Sure, there are some folks who'll hit it overnight, but let's both agree you and I are not that lucky. We gotta work for ours. When it looks like you'll never make it, push that much harder. When you think it's time to quit, sharpen your sword and swing with more power.

There's nothing different about you or any other

person making a million a year in your industry. Those who have hit it have just done the work. If you want an even faster way to get there, copy the people who've already done it and then do it faster than they did. The only reason you're not making seven figures a year right now is you. Your thinking and fears are the only limitations holding you back. It's time you Break Free!

If you'd like to get clear on what you need to do in order to hit your sales goals as well as the seven-figure mark, I'd suggest you check out my sales program www.showupandclose.com. You'll learn the million dollar sales process I use to close multiple prospects at once.

If you're ready to invest in your personal success and you'd like to find out about the programs we have developed especially for you, simply head over to www.HardcoreCloser.com/tribe and we'll have a sales conversation about your future.

Chapter 17

Three Reasons Salespeople Like to Blow Their Money

If you haven't met a broke salesman, you haven't met too many salesmen. We salesmen are notorious for blowing our money. Every sales manager in America has had to advance at least one of their top producers at some point. Even the guys who make millions in income per year can be cash broke.

We love to live on the edge. Most of us are addicted to taking risk. Risk with our bodies, our money and pretty much anything else we can risk. If it doesn't scare us and get our adrenaline flowing, we usually want no part of it. Stocks? CDs? No, you can keep those safe, yet boring investments. We want some risk involved with our shit.

What Fun is Making a Lot of Money if You Can't Blow It All?

Just because a salesman might be broke doesn't necessarily mean he's not a top producer either. Often, the biggest producer is the poorest bastard in the company. Top producing salespeople have no fear; this includes no fear of blowing their money and earning more.

Let's take a glance into the mind of a salesman and find out why in the hell they are rich on Friday and broke on Monday, every single week. One of my mentors once told me: "You can't overpay a salesman. They will always live above their means. The more money they make, the more money they blow." In my experience, this is true 99 percent of the time.

Why Do Salespeople Like to Blow Their Money?

#1: Confidence

Top producing salespeople are FULL of confidence. You can't be a closer without having an extreme amount of confidence. Confidence is mostly a good thing, but it can leave you high and dry, too. Salespeople are confident they can always earn more money. They know if they just close a few more sales, they can pay for whatever it is they just blew their money on.

When you've won award after award, closed sale after sale and have a ton of prospects in your pipeline, it's hard to think any dollar you have will be the last dollar you earn. Therefore, you blow cash like there's no end in sight, because oftentimes, there isn't.

#2: Staying Hungry

I've lived out most of my sales career trying to buy shit that kept me motivated to go make more money. If I had a fat bank account, I wouldn't have the desire to go earn more. I know me—I'll get lazy. I'll live off a fat bank account until it's gone. I need to invest, buy and keep the economy around me stimulated. I've gotten a lot better now, but in my past for every fat check I earned, I bought myself something nice. Cars, houses, you name it.

Staying hungry dates back to caveman days. If the caveman had a cave full of food, he had no desire to hunt. If you have a fat ass savings, there's no urgency to close a sale like you need it, because you don't. If your cave is empty, you're forced to go out and hunt for food. Evolution has traded full caves for full bank accounts. Many people need to stay hungry in order to hunt.

#3: Upper Limits

I first learned about upper limits in 2014, when I met a mentor who was really big on helping guys like me push through them. Prior to this experience, I didn't even know I had them. Upper limits are psychological limitations we (in most cases) unknowingly place on ourselves. In other words, if we have $10,000 in our bank account and we think we don't deserve it, we will drain that well dry.

Many of us grew up dirt poor and didn't have

parents who taught us how to manage a six and seven-figure income. Growing up this way often exposed us to phrases like: "Money is the root of all evil," and other crap. Even though consciously we know this is garbage, subconsciously it's planted deep within us. It all translates into: "You have too much money, so blow it, because you're not worthy of having this cash." We sales folk are a glutton for self-infliction.

What I've Learned about Saving Money in 20 Years as a Full-time Salesman

I know me. You need to get to know you. If you have an upper limit problem and you are tempted to blow money, blow it on investments, stocks, real estate and cars to flip. My neighbor bought a McLaren P1 , drove it for a year, sold it and made a million dollars in straight profit when he sold it. That's the type of money you need to condition yourself to spend.

Spend money with the intention of getting it back. Instead of strippers, drugs, bottle service and high fashion, spend it on cars you can flip and houses you can rent. It may be hard at first, but all habits have to form at some point.

If you're ready to invest in your personal success and you'd like to find out about the programs we have developed especially for you, simply head over to www.HardcoreCloser.com/tribe and we'll have a sales conversation about your future.

On some days, my blog is read 50,000 times, so we want to make sure we serve those who are 100 percent ready first. Thanks for cooperating. Also, don't forget to share this with your friends and fellow salespeople.

Chapter 18

Prospect CPR: Reviving Dead Leads

In sales, we say, "Buy or die," but that's rarely the case. Instead, what most sales professionals should say is: "Buy or I'll leave you to die." Let's get real, that's what usually happens. The salesman drops the ball. Then down the road, when the salesman who dropped the ball is replaced by "the new guy" it's up to "the new guy" to revive the ball dropper's old leads.

Reviving Dead Leads is a Quick Way to Make Some Sales

Most people, whether in sales or not, hate being rejected. It shuts them down. They don't know how to take it or react to it. The word "no" scares the hell out of people. Most folks will do anything they can in order to avoid hearing it. This includes letting good leads die by not following up properly. The fear of "no" leaves a wake of dead leads someone has to close up.

It might as well be you! I mean, if you're the new guy, or if you need to close some leads and get some extra sales in, you might as well take a crack at reviving dead leads. It's not as hard as it sounds, and the prospect most likely knows about your product or service. Dead leads are kind of like warm leads, and they are far from cold leads.

Do Some CPR on Dead Leads and Watch What Happens

In case you haven't caught on yet, I use CPR as an acronym for my old lead selling process. You can't go after dead leads in the same fashion you go after new leads. You can never be 100 percent sure what's been told to the prospect in the past, or how poorly their previous experience went.

When I started my first day selling cars, the manager gave me a stack of old leads. He said, "Get after it. Make some calls." That was about the extent of his advice. I had no idea what these leads were all about. He could have given me the pissed off customer list for all I knew. I was no rookie, though; I already had a plan. A plan that worked so good and so fast, I was bumped to Internet leads in two days.

Reframe the Context of the Conversation

Before I list out the steps to reviving dead leads, you need to position yourself properly in order for my strategy to work. You see, you don't know the mind frame of the dead lead. You've got to come in as a Trojan horse, not a charging army. The way to do this is by calling with questions. Let the prospect know you're from the "Customer Satisfaction Department" and you're there to make them happy. There's no need to say anything about sales at this point. Just this small exchange of words will get the prospect to drop their guard a lot more easily.

These days, most sales reps' titles aren't "XYZ Sales" anyway. We have names like "customer service rep" or "client experience consultant." Your first job is to find out the proper information to arm you with the facts you need, in order to make your lead an irresistible offer.

Revive old, dead, stale leads in three easy steps

C – *Contact*

I don't just call old leads. Matter of fact, before I call anyone, I text them, so they know who I am and why I'm calling. I beat caller ID at its own game. Look at it this way; if someone was dying, I'd do everything I could CPR-wise to bring them back to life. These dying leads get treated the same way. I will text, email and call them until I get them back to life. *Don't you die on me John Doe at 867-5309.* You owe it to the prospect to reach out to them in every way you can. I even reach out via social media. I'll tweet a prospect or DM one. Whatever it takes.

P – *Problem Search*

Your job in this step is to search for the problems to confront. To be clear, there's more than one problem that must be solved. The first problem is that they are a dead lead. The second problem is the challenge they are facing, that your services can solve. Find out what you need to solve by asking questions. I have 6-10 prewritten questions for every dead lead. People don't seem to mind taking a "survey for the Customer Satisfaction Department." I use the feedback from the answers of their questions to solve their problems.

R – Recommend the Solution

Of course, the recommendation is your product, but you've got to position it properly. After they drop their guard, answer your questions and in the process, tell you their problems, you make the offer to solve those problems with your services or products. If you've done the second step of this process properly, it's the easiest one to execute.

There you have it, three steps to revive dead leads from beyond the grave. All it takes is a little finesse on your end and you, asking the right questions. The next thing you know, you've got coffee—because coffee is for closers. If you're looking for more in-depth training on my CPR and CATCH selling systems, check out www.showupandclose.com. The program will change your sales, your business and ultimately your life.

If you're ready to invest in your personal success and you'd like to find out about the programs we have developed especially for you, simply head over to www.HardcoreCloser.com/tribe and we'll have a sales conversation about your future.

Chapter 19

Six Reasons Why Salespeople Don't Contact or Follow Up with Leads

According to the late, great Chet Holmes, in order to make a sale, you'll need to follow up with a prospect twelve times, eight of whom will tell you, "No." "No" is the natural enemy of the salesman. Most humans fear their enemy. Therefore, most salespeople are scared to follow up. How's that for lineage?

Most Salespeople Are Scared of the Word "No"

The word "no" to most, means the sale is dead. There's no money to be made and it's a loss. By nature, salesmen are competitive and hate to lose. Losing is painful to most of us. Humans will do damn near anything to avoid pain. Knowing there's a possibility of that pain becoming real, salespeople will work harder to avoid "no" than they will to hear "yes."

Follow up takes skill!

If you know up front it's going to take twelve contacts with eight of them a resounding "No," then it allows you to get your head right. Most salespeople have a firm belief they will have a one-call close or nothing. Then they always seem shocked when the prospect buys from someone with strong follow up skills.

What's worse are the salespeople who don't even bother to call leads at all. I've been running an event called Break Free Academy for around two years now. BFA is a two-day event where I help salesmen create funnels to capture leads. Some of the BFA attendees generate leads for their referral partners. The number one complaint these attendees have is that their referral partners don't even bother to contact their leads.

It Amazes Me, All the Money Salespeople Leave on the Table by Not Calling and Doing Any Follow Up with Leads.

When you start thinking of leads as money, and not just sales, your perspective will shift. Each lead a salesperson receives costs money to obtain. Each lead also has the potential to generate a positive ROI for the cost spent to get it. When you start looking at your leads as wins and losses in regards to money, you'll see the real value in follow up.

Over 100 attendees have graduated from Break Free Academy. Recently, we held a reunion event at my office in Dallas. While at the event, we discussed leads from contact to close. Turns out there are some pretty common reasons why salespeople don't contact or follow up with leads. Yes, to most of us it's baffling, but apparently, it's a real problem.

Not Following Up with Leads is a Serious Industry Issue

Not closing or even following up with leads hurts everyone. It hurts the lead, because they obviously became a lead to get help, and if you don't help them you hurt them. It hurts the company because they paid for a lost lead. It also hurts the salesperson because they haven't earned the money they should have.

Here are six reasons sales people don't contact or follow up with leads:

#1: They Don't Have a System to Follow up with Leads

When you give your people leads, do you show them how the lead came into your ecosystem? Do you walk your salespeople/referral partners through the process you've gone through to get those leads? Most salespeople are afraid to call or follow up with leads because they don't want to look dumb. So, instead of seeking wisdom they just avoid the lead altogether.

If you generate leads for a team, employees or partners, you need to design a clear selling and follow up process for them. Take the time to educate them on how leads are generated and what steps they need to take next. Once YOU take the lead with the leads, set expectations with your selling systems you have put into place and get your team to agree to it. When they receive clarity, they will become less fearful of appearing dumb to the prospect, and they will be more likely to do what you deem needs to be done.

#2: They Have New Leads to Distract Them

"But if I have new leads coming in every day, why do I need to follow up with the ones I didn't close?" Believe it or not, I used to say this all the time. I used to be a "one and done" lead churn and burn guy. I had so many new leads coming in, I wasn't worried about backtracking with follow up. That was until I saw the actual dollar amount I was missing out on by not following up.

The problem for many is that they are so focused on new leads they don't have time to follow up with past leads. This is when email automation comes into play. If you truly don't have time to follow up, set up automatic follow up systems to do it for you. There's too much money in follow up not to be doing it.

#3: They are Scared of "No"

Humans will do damn near anything to avoid pain. The word "no" is such a serious word. By definition it's absolutely negative. No one likes to hear it, see it, or even know it's coming. If it takes eight times hearing the word "no" to get one "YES!" and most salespeople stop at the first "no," what does that say about fear? In reality, "no" is just a word. It's not permanent and in most cases "no" means "I'm not 100 percent clear on what you are proposing, so I'll protect myself with 'NO.'"

Most prospects will say "No" just to avoid making a decision. Most salespeople take that "No" as a permanent answer. You've got to be a professional mind changer. Prospects say "No" for many reasons and most of them are complete bullshit. It's your job to clear out the BS and get the prospect clear on your offer, so they can say "YES!" Don't fear the "NO," work your ass off for the "YES!"

#4: They Haven't Earned the Right to Follow-Up

Salespeople blow it on first impressions every day. Many don't even know how shitty their 10-second elevator pitch really is. I've seen guys talk their way right out of a lay down sale. I've also seen guys blow sales that even I couldn't come back and save. When this happens it's guaranteed the salesperson won't follow up. Even worse, this flub is now in their head and it affects them on how they contact the next lead.

Vicious cycle…

Worse yet, when a salesman offers no value to the prospect and they know it, they fear the follow up. The pain of hearing the word "no" is real. When a sales rep hears it once, they will do damn near anything to not hear it again. That includes not contacting or following up their leads. You have to earn the right to hear "YES." That comes by being an expert, showing value through demonstration and solving the prospect's problem. If these steps aren't ALL taken, you've blown the sale.

#5: *They Don't Want to Seem Desperate or Pushy*

The salesperson's ego is delicate. We rely so much on our ego and confidence that most of us will avoid damaging it. Salespeople hate to look desperate or needy. No one ever closed an earned deal by begging. Beggars want free stuff. You gotta pay the cost to close a sale. The ego can cost a salesman a fortune. We also want to appear successful in our own right. The ego won't let you be successful and desperate at the same time.

The average salesman's ego can be crushed pretty easily. If they seem needy and come off as pushy, they fear the prospect won't talk to them or ever buy from them. So, instead of taking the shot and doing follow up, they just avoid the prospect altogether in hopes the prospect might reach back out to them. Just a heads up: *it never works like that.*

#6: They Didn't Pay for the Lead

This one pisses me off the most. I've worked for companies that supplied leads for us. In exchange for supplying leads, you take a smaller commission split. I looked at this as if I were paying for the leads and every deal counted. Yet, I watched lots of sales guys not give AF because they didn't have a monetary investment in obtaining the lead (in their mind.)

If you're lucky enough to get leads handed to you, you work the hell out of each one and thank the person who gave them to you! There are so many salespeople out there who are spending their time, their money and putting in major effort to get leads every day. If you have them handed to you and you don't contact or follow up, you're an entitled asshat. Yeah, I said it. Let that sink in for a few…

I may have just listed six reasons sales people don't contact or follow up with leads, but there's really no excuse for not doing so. Leads are the lifeblood of sales. Without contacts and prospects, we are nothing. You can't close what you don't have. If you don't have leads, you're not closing. It's that simple. Leads pay your bills. Each one represents a dollar amount. It should be in your blood to go get those dollars or you should go get an engineering job with HR.

Registration for Break Free Academy is always open. Come spend two days in Dallas, Texas with me. We will work hand in hand to create a lead-generating sales funnel and set up killer follow up systems to maximize every one of the leads the funnels will get you. Apply at www.bfadigital.com.

If you're ready to invest in your personal success and you'd like to find out about the programs we have developed especially for you, simply head over to www.HardcoreCloser.com/tribe and we'll have a sales conversation about your future.

Chapter 20

How to Relentlessly Follow Up with Prospects Without Annoying Them and Blowing the Sale

You left the meeting and had a good feeling about this one. He said to follow up with him in the next few days and he'll close the deal with you. You need the sale. You know the prospect is a busy man. You've already left a few messages and sent an email or two.

How much follow-up is too much?

There's a fine, really fine line between follow up and annoyance. There's also a weird part of the process where annoyances become follow up and the prospect respects your hustle. Oh, and that part about them getting mad and telling you to never to contact them again? That happens too.

The last thing any of us wants to do is piss off a prospect by bugging them too much. The first thing any of us wants to do is make a sale. Both are valid consequences of follow up. It's your job as a salesman to know exactly how much follow up is the right amount. If you're not sure, it's cool, stick with me and I'll teach you how I do it.

If You're Gonna Close Sales, You've Got to Relentlessly Follow Up

Relentless follow up doesn't have to be annoying. It doesn't have to piss the prospect off. If you do it right, the prospect will love your follow up and close with you when the time is right. It's all in the technique you use and the perception of that technique by the prospect.

I've sold cars, homes and everything in-between at some point in my life. I've had several sales "jobs" that required me to do daily follow up with prospects who weren't exactly happy to be bothered so frequently. I don't do well with "no," so I had to concoct some creative ways to get myself back in front of the prospect every day to do my job and close the sale.

The car business probably required the most follow up of any job I've ever had. Selling cars is a "right now" business. If you don't close them "right now," your prospect most likely won't be back. If a prospect leaves the dealership, you've got to be one BAMF on your follow up to get them back to the barn.

People don't really care too much for salesmen, let alone car salesmen. That said, prospects don't appreciate a car salesman calling, emailing and texting them every day. When I had to do so in order to feed my family, I had to figure out a way to follow up, get them back to the dealership and close them without pissing them off to where they'd go buy from my competitor.

If a Prospect Walked, I had a Surefire Way to Entice Them to Finish the Deal

I do everything in my life with intent. I'm not fearful of consequences, good or bad. Most people don't have intentions. If you have intentions, you have consequences. Most people run from consequences and avoid doing anything intentionally. Because of this, a lot of the people you meet won't expect you to have intent. They will almost always assume other people will think and act the same they do. When you're different, you make the sale.

I believe it takes 12 touches to entice someone to buy. In my business, the average prospect reads my shit and watches me for eight months before they make a buying decision. It takes me getting in front of you a shit ton of times before you'll actually buy from me. I'm okay with that. If you think about it, you reading this right now is me following up with you. Doesn't really seem like it, though does it?

Exactly!

Here's how to creatively follow up with prospects in a way that makes them buy from you:

Day 1:

You just met the prospect. You had a good sales conversation and you need to follow up. As soon as you get off the phone or get back to your car, if it was an in-person meeting, send them an email. Not just any email, an email with something you mentioned in the meeting that you thought they would like.

During the initial meeting (phone or in-person) I mention a third-party service or review that will help them, not me. This shows them I care about them and that I have expert information for them. I make them want this during the meeting, so they'll look forward to getting the email from me with the information.

Day 2:

I call them up and double check to make sure they got my email yesterday. I also tell them I enjoyed meeting them yesterday. I never thank them for their time. My time is just as valuable as theirs in my mind. If I thank them, that means they did me a favor. By telling them I enjoyed meeting them it puts me on their level subconsciously.

I also give them the heads up I have some more cool stuff they will like, so I warn them to be on the lookout for my emails. I want them hanging and expecting my contacts, so that when they happen it's anticipated. It's almost like setting another meeting with them.

Day 3:

I send another email with more cool information to either reinforce or add to the info I sent them on day one. "*Oh, hey by the way, I found this video that's perfect for you.*" I'm following up, but with more stuff they want. I haven't asked for the sale again yet. I'm simply doing what I call "stacking the good." This means I'm giving them a ton of value and demonstrating my use and expertise at the same time.

The law of reciprocity is a real thing. If I do enough cool stuff for a prospect that brings value to their life, they will want to restore order and give value to my life. Most times this is in the form of a sale. They buy from me because they feel like they owe it to me.

Day 4:

On this day, I'll send a video I've personally made for them. Really, I've made it for everyone, but it seems as if it's just for them. On this video, I'll give value and show social proof of the results the prospect wants. In other words, I might show them testimonials or examples of current and past clients who have gotten the results the prospect wants.

At the end of this video I ask for their business through a clear, strong and precise call to action. At this point, they have a really good idea if I'm their guy or not. The decision has to be made. My call to action gives them a time period in which to reply to me. They have to reach out with an answer of either "Yes" or "No."

Day 5:

I follow up and make sure they got the video from yesterday. If I have to leave a voicemail, I do so as well and send the same message via text. I want them to feel like the video is super important, that they have a sense of urgency to watch it. It's as if the video is expiring or going away soon.

I'm not asking for business on this call. If I do get them on the phone instead of going to voicemail, I hit them with a call to action just like the video. Not begging for the sale, but insisting they need to make a decision of "Yes" or "No."

Day 6:

They get another email from me. This email explains I've been trying to catch them so we can close our business and get started moving forward. I highlight what was in the previous emails, how it benefits them and how what I sell can solve their problems. I also point out that a week has already passed. And in doing so, make them feel six days behind.

This email is full of scarcity, sales pitches and benefits just waiting for them, which will be theirs as soon as they take action. This is also the first time I've aggressively asked for the business. This email needs to lay it all out to them. Be firm, but empathetic.

Days 7 – 10:

I make them miss me. They've gotten value, follow up and an aggressive sales pitch via email from me, so I'll give them a break. Take the scarcity to a new level. Act as if I don't need them. They'll think I've moved on, but again, I'm operating with intent. They have no clue.

Day 11:

I call them and make sure they are all good. Most times it's a voicemail and text they get. Any time I call the phone and leave a VM, I send the same message via text. This is why it's important to always get the mobile number, not the office number. I let them know I'm here for them and ready to make it happen when they are. Keep it short and simple.

This call is simply a checkup. I let them know I'll be sending another important video tomorrow via email. The purpose of this text and VM is 100 percent to set the hook for tomorrow's follow up video.

Day 12:

This will be the last "real" follow up they get from me. I'll send them the video I mentioned in yesterday's text and voicemail. This video simply states that it's been two weeks since we first got into contact. When I show them the results of other clients after two weeks with me, I make them feel the pain of what they are missing out on, using social proof all the way.

I also let them know I'm gonna let them off the hook. I'll get off their ass for now. I reassure the excuses they are thinking, such as being busy, not ready, etc., I'm empathetic but at the same time I show them what it's costing not to get this done.

After the 12 days, I start following up via email once a week and phone call/text every two weeks. Any time I have something of value for them, I send it at those times and follow up. I keep them in long-term, weekly follow up mode until they decide to reach back out to me. I don't put much more time or focus on them.

You can easily incorporate this same intentional process into your follow up. More times than not, the prospect will buy from you at the fourth or eighth follow up. Rarely do I have to go the distance for 12 days. It's all a matter of expert positioning on your end. Prospects buy from experts at 3X the rate they buy from salespeople.

If you're ready to implement a sales system that allows you to have seemingly casual, yet powerful sales conversations that lead to closing three out of five inbound sales calls, I got you. Use my program www.inboundleadcloser.com and get the tools and the sales system you need to assist you in closing more sales.

If you're ready to invest in your personal success and you'd like to find out about the programs we have developed especially for you, simply head over to www.HardcoreCloser.com/tribe and we'll have a sales conversation about your future.

Chapter 21

The Secret Behind the Two Step Upsell Strategy

"Would you like fries with that?" has probably made more money than any other phrase ever crafted by a salesman. This sentence is pure sales genius. It's a simple script any order taker can memorize in seconds. The best part about it is it doesn't even seem like a sales pitch.

McDonald's famous phrase "Would you like fries with that?" is a shining example of what I call the "two step upsell" or TSU for short. The TSU is often overlooked by salespeople and business owners. At the same time, it's exactly what has allowed McDonalds to dominate the food scene with a mediocre product for decades.

This same, simple upsell process can be introduced into your business, too. And no, it doesn't matter what you sell. If you have more than one product or service, you should offer an upsell package. If you're not making the offer, you're not making the money.

Every Business Should Have an Easy to Implement Upsell Strategy

Here's what happens in most scenarios. A guy walks

into a store and sees a pair of $500 shoes he really likes. You mention they look great on him and he decides to buy. Most salespeople stop right there and pat themselves on the back. This common practice not only hurts the company; it hurts the salesman's commission check.

The right thing for the salesman to do would be to offer the customer a matching high-end belt and wallet to go along with his shoes. He's already in the buying mood; he clearly has money to spend or he wouldn't be buying $500 shoes. It's the perfect storm to suck as much money out of him as he wants to give you.

Clients like this LOVE to spend their money. They get a small high from buying high-end goods. It's nice to know you can spend some serious cash and get treated like a king.

The Two Step Upsell Strategy Works in Pretty Much Every Business

If your company offers more than one product or service, you should make multiple offers to each buyer no matter how much you think they won't buy. Not everyone thinks like you. If you only offer one service or product, you need to look into creating a bolt-on service or product that you can use for an upsell. Every company needs more than one offer.

The best time to get folks to spend even more is when they are already buying. I'm not saying rip people off, take advantage of people, or anything like that. I'm saying if you see me in the store buying a suit, sell me a tie and a shirt to match. If you don't offer, I won't ask, but you're doing both of us a disservice by not asking.

If you're a manager or business owner, you need to train your people to always, always, always offer a two step upsell. The TSU is really simple. Matter of fact, like most aspects of sales, the simpler you keep the TSU and the script to match, the more you will sell. Think "Would you like fries with that?"

Implementing a Two Step Upsell Strategy into Your Business Can Increase Profitability by 50 Percent or More

Here's how the TSU works. It's not hard. It just has to be done. The offer has to be made. If there is no offer made to the customer, there is no chance of a sale. You have to ask for the business in order to get it. You know all those items at the counter at 7-Eleven? Yeah, the trinkets and candy stuff. When's the last time the clerk asked you if you wanted one? I know if they started asking if I wanted a Kit Kat I'd probably buy one. That's a chance at a dollar more out of every customer who buys. Yet, they never ask.

Step #1 of the TSU is simple. Once the customer has made the decision to spend money and become a customer, you simple ask if they would enjoy something else you sell that goes along with their needs; nothing more, nothing less. "Sir, we have a great belt and wallet combo that pairs perfectly with those shoes. Would you like me to grab them for you? What size belt do you wear?"

Step #2 of the TSU is to take their money. Yep that's it. Make an offer and collect the payment from those who take you up on it. I told you, in sales, keeping it simple works best.

Just Two Steps: 1) make the offer and 2) collect the payment.

If you're missing out on sales by not implementing actions like TSU into your sales regimen, I'll teach you how to take knowledge and turn it into action. My sales program will expand your mind and allow you to increase closing ratios without being such a pushy a-hole. Check out Show Up and Close at www.showupandclose.com.

If you're ready to invest in your personal success and you'd like to find out about the programs we have developed especially for you, simply head over to www.HardcoreCloser.com/tribe and we'll have a sales conversation about your future.

Chapter 22

How to Ask for Referrals in a Way that Gets Clients to Send You Everyone They Know

We're constantly told to ask for referrals. Referrals are the lifeblood of many of our businesses. Referrals are free, come already programmed by third party social proof and are generally easy to close. Matter of fact, most referrals are straight up lay down sales. Yet, so many salespeople drop the ball when it comes to asking their clients to send them more clients.

Why are So Many Salespeople Afraid to Ask for Referrals?

Let's be honest, if you're reading this you're most likely an above average salesman. That means you've seen the average and below average salesmen screw up deals in ways you could have never imagined. If we're above average, that means there are a lot of people who have a skill set subpar to ours. Those people don't feel very confident about their abilities and screw up sales. This makes them afraid to ask for referrals because when the client says "No," they are then faced with the reality of how bad the job they did was.

Another reason salespeople drop the ball when it

comes to referrals is due to insecurity. The average salesperson gets surprised and excited when they make a sale. Oftentimes, after it's closed, they can't believe they made a sale. It's a lot for the mediocre to handle. They don't want to *blow their high* by asking for a referral and being told, "No."

The key to getting referrals from happy clients is knowing exactly how to ask for referrals. If you've done a good job for your customer, it's only logical you'll offer to do a good job for their sphere of influence. Still many salespeople leave money on the table every day by not asking.

Ask for Referrals Like They Owe Them to You

What's even crazier is that referrals are the easiest leads to get. It's all about positioning your prospect to send you referrals from the beginning of the process. It all starts with the service. If you treat the client you have like gold, they will have no problem sending their friends to you to be treated like gold, too. Think about it. It makes them look good if they send you referrals and their friends think you're as awesome as they do.

Start the sales process out by treating the prospect like gold. Be available, knowledgeable and the expert solution provider to their problem. Treat them like the dollar sign they represent. By doing this, they will already be thinking of friends and people they know who'd enjoy your service like they are.

By doing your job to the best of your ability, they will already start the referral process internally. When you close them and ask for referrals, they'll have already thought about who they can send you. If a prospect feels you're the expert and the best they've ever seen at what you do, they will have no problem sending everyone they know to you.

Knowing the Right Time to Ask for Referrals is Crucial

You've got to pump clients for referrals when they are on cloud nine. Right after they are happy with the buying decision they just made with you, that's when you ask if they have any friends you can make as happy as they are right now. They'll let you know exactly who they know who would love the same outcome.

I've been the referral king in every industry I've worked in. Cars, homes, loans, consulting and car washing, it didn't matter where I worked. I worked for referrals. I've always had a pretty easy-to-follow system for asking for referrals. Even the script is super simple to memorize. Don't ever knock simplicity. The simpler something is, the better it will work.

Here's the Process I Use So My Clients Will Send Me Everyone They Know:

First off, when the sale begins, I prep them up front. Early on in the sales conversation, I simply say with 100 percent confidence:

"I'm here to help you end your search and make an informed buying decision today. I'm on your team and gonna treat you better than you've been treated at any similar place before. Know why? Because I don't just want to make you happy, I want to make everyone you know happy. You'll see how much I care as we go through the process."

Looking someone in the eye and telling them you're gonna do the best job for them they've ever seen is powerful. Most people are not bold enough to make this claim. But when you follow through on it, it further sinks in with them how good you really are.

Second, I after I close the sale and they are ecstatic with their decision, I hit them in the heat of the moment with this:

"Earlier, I told you I was going to do the best job for you that you've ever seen. Did I exceed your expectations? Great, I work on referrals. Wouldn't you like your friends and family to be as happy as you are right now when they need this product? Simply take two minutes to write down three recommendations and introductions you can make for me and I'll treat them exactly like I've treated you."

Positioning your words in the manner of the above word track will set them up to send you people because A: they are happy; B: they have confidence in you to not screw their friends over. You've just become their go-to guy for whatever it is you sell.

Referrals are horizontal lead sources. Each referral can lead to 3-10 more referrals and so on and so on. Becoming an expert at asking for referrals will make you rich. Effectively generating leads from referrals is a long lost art in sales these days. Most salespeople even forget to ask for referrals from Internet leads.

If You Work Referrals Hard Enough, You'll Never Have to Buy Leads.

If you're looking for a sales program for you or your team that will embolden you enough to close deals, ask for referrals and serve your prospects better than any of your competitors, I've got the perfect one. Check out www.inboundleadcloser.com. It will turn anyone into a sales machine.

If you're ready to invest in your personal success and you'd like to find out about the programs we

have developed especially for you, simply head over to www.HardcoreCloser.com/tribe and we'll have a sales conversation about your future.

Chapter 23

How to Turn One-time Clients into Repeat Customers

Starbucks, Cici's Pizza and Chick-fil-A all have one thing in common that make them the best at what they do. No, it's not making the most delicious coffee, pizza, or chicken. It's that they make sure to say, "Hello, welcome to (company name)" the second anyone enters through the door. All three acknowledge you and make you feel important the moment you set foot into their establishments.

Money is not easy to come by. We ALL work really hard for it, no matter how much we have. We continually spend money in the places that make us feel good about spending it. I'm more apt to be a repeat customer in an establishment with mediocre products but excellent service, more than I am the opposite.

We like being treated well when we spend our money. We've all seen great businesses come and go. Yet, that diner up the street with Charlene at the front door greeting every person who walks in, has crappy food, but excellent service and has, through no coincidence, been open for four decades. Meanwhile, the best steakhouse in town just closed shop.

Service Makes or Breaks a Business

We all pay so much and work so hard to get each customer. The key to running a profitable and sustainable business is to turn one-time customers into repeat customers. If you treat them like the gold they are, they will continue to pay their gold for your services. If you treat them like shit, they won't give you shit for repeat business. OR referrals!

Ask any great business consultant how to increase profits easily and they will tell you to find a way to repeat sales to the already existing customer database. The cost of acquiring a new client vs. selling a complementary service to an existing one is the difference between staying in business or going out. If you're constantly working to get new people to buy your stuff, you're constantly paying for traffic. It cuts into your margins like a hot knife through butter.

The other sales equation that service helps out with is getting referrals. Maybe you sell a service like real estate or mortgages. People generally only need your help once every 5-10 years, so they can't repeat that often. They can tell all their friends about you and send them to you. It's new business you get for free, due to your superior service delivery.

Referrals won't happen without great service. Just like repeat customers won't happen if you treat them wrong. These days, so many businesses treat prospects like they don't need them. It doesn't take long for word of mouth to spread and people to decide they don't need the business.

Negative service gets more attention than positive service. Very few people love a place so much that they will go on Yelp and review it. Yet, that same person, once upset, will create a Yelp account just to warn others of how bad things were for them.

Fight 10 Times Harder for Good Service Publicity Than Bad Service Publicity

It all stems from our reptilian fight or flight mechanism. When we get bad service, it's in our DNA to warn others in our circles of the danger. When we receive good service, we take it as what we are supposed to get, and we may never mention it to anybody we know.

Some of the best service-delivering businesses offer discounts to repeat customers. You've seen punch cards, coupons and Starbucks does that deal where you can bring your receipt back later that day for a discounted second daily visit. The more you can get the same person to repeat business with you, the more each customer is worth to you. That's why Starbucks welcomes everyone that comes in, even when you don't buy a drink.

The question now is: *Do you provide Grade A service to every single person who comes in to your establishment?* Even with my business that I operate 100 percent online, I treat every prospect and customer like gold, giving them all sorts of great service. Greeting them by video, following up and rewarding them via email and so on. Even though clients may not walk into your office and you may not speak to them, you can still give them superior service with the right systems in place.

There are three keys to running and maintaining a super successful business. Service, upsells and referrals, those three things all fuel each other and create a synergy that propels a business into perpetual momentum. To put it simply, service sells. The better the service, the more the clientele will spend.

We Love Being Treated Well for Spending Money.

We work so hard for it; we deserve the best when we're buying. Maybe it's time for you to take inventory and see where you can step up your service game. How could you increase the customer experience? How can you make them want to come back and pay you as often as possible? How could you convert them into raving fans who send referrals on a regular basis? Figure those things out, implement them, and then watch profits increase dramatically.

If you're in sales, you're in service. Selling is one thing, but creating the experience is another. My sales program Show Up and Close will teach you how to close sales as you make clients feel like a million bucks. So, clients will come back to you and send all their friends your way as well. Check it out at www.showupandclose.com.

If you're ready to invest in your personal success and you'd like to find out about the programs we have developed especially for you, simply head over to www.HardcoreCloser.com/tribe and we'll have a sales conversation about your future.

Chapter 24

Three Ways to Step Up Your Negotiation Game

The art of negotiation is not to be taken lightly. Matter of fact, if you do take it lightly, you'll end up short of money. When you're in sales, you're always looking to maximize the commissions you can earn. Being a bad negotiator puts those commissions in jeopardy.

No one wants to miss out on money they've worked hard for. With that said, many people suck at negotiations and there's no telling how many billions in commissions are lost each year as a direct result.

Try and think of your sales negotiations as hostile hostage situations where you can't let the sale die. Your sale is being held hostage by your prospect and if you let it die, everyone loses.

As salesmen, we tend to overlook each sale and think it's no big deal if we don't close this one. Truth is, those no-big-deal misses make up for some pretty monstrous losses. If you blow a sale a week, you've missed 52 sales a year. That shit adds up quick.

To protect your sale, you need to stay sharp when it

comes to negotiating the deal and closing the tougher prospects. There are plenty of awesome sites with killer info on how to do this. There's also a bunch of books written by police and FBI hostage negotiators. I've read a lot of them and it really only comes down to three things.

#1: Don't Be Scared to Lose the Deal

We've all been there…on the buying side of a negotiation…and lost. Oh, the sadness. That sales guy must have seen our buying desire even though we tried like hell to hide it, even though the salesman seemed to have ice water in his veins.

It's funny how we will blow off a sale over some dumb shit, but at the same time don't want to lose one while negotiating. This is especially evident when we NEED a sale. We become the worst negotiators when we have to have that next deal.

If the prospect senses they can get over on you and that you're scared to lose them, they'll exploit you into a zero sum commission check. You don't want that do you? All that selling and no money to show for it. Say it ain't so. Don't let the prospect know you need them.

#2: Don't Let Your Emotions Get the Best of You

Anger, frustration, sadness and anxiety can kill your sales, your paycheck and even your credit score. Prospects these days will test you, too. They know if you blow your cool, they'll get a deal. They also know if you look anxious, they got you where they want you.

The *ONLY* emotion you need in the negotiation process is happiness. You'll sell more with a smile than you'll ever sell without one. Hell, you can damn near say anything as long as you're happy and smiling while it's said.

Negotiations can get steamy. Even if the prospect gets out of control, stay focused and smile. If the prospect is showing signs of emotions, that means you're winning the negotiations. Keep calm and close.

#3: Assume the Other Person Will Stop at Nothing to Get Their Way

In any competition, you've just got to assume the other team will stop at nothing to beat you. It's *ONLY* with this mentality that you stand a chance of winning. Why? Because 9 times out of 10, it's true.

Assuming the other party is relentless, means understanding they may get emotional, irrational and shady. You've got to be ready for all of this. You've also got to be equally as ruthless. Not mean, not shady, but not willing to relent on your side. This works even better when you let the other side feel as if you're on their team.

Humans love getting their way. Most of the spoiled ones will whine and cry until they do get their way. This can wear and tear on us salesmen, but if we let our guard down for one minute; we can lose a deal. Stay in the conversation and out of your head, and you'll pick up on their little tricks and tests.

If you sell real estate, mortgage loans, insurance products, stocks or anything else, the general public is going to try and get you to lower the price of your shit. The only way you can protect your check and make sure you're always closing is to get better at negotiating your costs.

In the initial contact, position yourself as a person who doesn't negotiate, but if that doesn't work, don't blow the sale because of scarcity, emotions, or relenting. I'd love to help you win more of the commission checks you're working your ass off for.

If you're ready to invest in your personal success and you'd like to find out about the programs we have developed especially for you, simply head over to www.HardcoreCloser.com/tribe and we'll have a sales conversation about your future.

Chapter 25

How to Convert Your Competition into Your Biggest Lead Source

I used to think I had to hate my competition. I looked at every market I entered as me vs. them. That stinking thinking has costs me millions of dollars. Yeah, I said it. Most people won't tell you the areas they failed because they're too busy talking about how awesome they are. Not here. You get the facts only from me. It ain't always rainbows and sunshine in Closerland.

My ignorance, arrogance and hardheadedness have killed income I could have used to further push my business agenda. I've talked shit, trolled and berated some of my competitors. I've always had a burn-the-bridges mentality. I've always felt like I need to force myself to work. Going straight at my competitors has forced me to outwork them.

Your Competition Can Easily Become Your Biggest Lead Source.

I'm a hardhead who's always done hardscrabble work to make my place. I don't know why I tend to do it that way. Maybe it's my Alpha warrior personality type. Either way it's a dumbshit way to do business. I'm telling you now, it's easier and more profitable to work *with* your competitors than to compete *against* them.

A few years back, I was listening to some guy at a real estate event talk about broker-to-broker selling. He said, "Do you know who an agent's best client is? Another agent. You do not compete with each other. You collaborate." It made complete sense to me. If an agent has a listing, another agent brings the buyer and vice versa. The same principle applies to your business, too.

It Takes an Abundance Mentality to Do Business This Way

I get trade referrals these days from many of my would-be competitors. They send me clients and vice versa. These guys and gals all teach similar stuff as I do. They look for clients in the same industry, too. The reason we collaborate instead of compete is simple. We know EXACTLY who we want to work with.

Knowing exactly who it is you can help allows you to get clear on exactly who you can't help. Every business has prospects they can't serve. Oftentimes, when Company A can't help someone, Company B can. These two can trade business and profitably serve the public in a major way.

I've got three or four other sales trainers who I send

prospects to. They send me the type of person I'm looking for as well. We are all clear on who we want to help. If they don't fit my programs, I send them to a competitor who CAN help them. Then I ask for referrals.

Instead of thinking small and scrambling for every lead we get, we think big—on the level of serving the community—not closing sales. This allows us to get the right help for the right people. Think about doctors. Doctors refer each other all the time. Even to the point of referring you to a competitor for a second opinion. They ALL still make money and they ALL still serve the community as a whole; they don't just look out for themselves.

Collectively Serving the Entire Community Allows You to Gain More Referrals and Close More Sales.

The way to convert your competition into your biggest lead source is to lead them. Next time you have a prospect who's not a fit for you, but who is a good fit for the competition, call the competing company and offer them the lead. Explain to them that from time to time this happens and you'd like to trust them to take good care of your people.

After they close the lead you send, hit them up and let them know what it is that you sell and what you look for in a prospect. Most of the time they will be more than happy to strike up a relationship with you. Just be sure they treat your prospects as well as you treat theirs. Explain what you expect and get all that out of the way up front.

I learned I'm not for everyone, early on in my career. Prospects looking for a feel good message will hate me. If they are seeking a guy in a suit who goes to church on Sundays, they won't like me. There are plenty of sales trainers out there who are clean-cut, suit-wearing, God-fearing Christians. I'd rather refer my prospects to one of those types of sales trainers than leave them hanging.

Meanwhile, if prospects are looking for a brutal truth-telling, cuss-like-a-sailor, tattooed, real-ass person to get honest with them, I'm their guy. Both types of prospects exist. Those who buy from one may not buy from the other. Why not collaborate and sell what you can to both? Turn every lead into something.

Instead of bashing, hating and fighting your competitors, collaborate with them. You'll serve the entire community and close more sales. It's that easy. Don't do what I did and miss out on millions due to ego. If I could go back, I'd make amends with a lot of people I started shit with.

I Didn't Know There was a Better, Easier Way to Get Leads from Competitors

I thought that in order for me to get leads from the competition, I had to advertise where they did and target their followers, when all along we could have been growing together, serving ONLY our clients with best results. I'll never make that mistake again and I'd warn you against it as well.

If you're ready to implement a sales system that allows you to have seemingly casual, yet powerful sales conversations that lead to closing three out of five inbound sales calls, I got you. Check out my program www.inboundleadcloser.com. It will give you the tools and sales system you need to assist you in closing more sales.

If you're ready to invest in your personal success and you'd like to find out about the programs we have developed especially for you, simply head over to www.HardcoreCloser.com/tribe and we'll have a sales conversation about your future.

Chapter 26

How to Prospect AND Close Via Facebook Chat

In my opinion, the less time you spend on the phone, the more money you make. I know that's contradictional (my word) to what we are normally told and taught in this industry. If you'll hear me out, though, I will enlighten you as to why I feel this way and why this way of thinking has been worth a seven-figure income to me.

Before you learn how to prospect and close via Facebook chat, you've got to know why it's an important sales skill to possess. The same principles I'm going to teach you pertaining to chat, will also work via text message and email. In a world where phone calls go unanswered almost 90 percent of the time, it's important to learn to write.

Those of us who can write are the future. Learning to be just as effective in text as you are face-to-face is crucial if you want to remain a top producer for the next 10 years. Every day, I have more and more people tell me how they are reaching prospects via text message and Facebook chat, more than on the phone. Texting is not going anywhere, so you might as well adapt.

Now, let's talk about the benefits of selling via text.

If you can write as well as you speak, you'll be able to give your pitch even more smoothly. Those of us who can write make the best videos, public presentations and face-to-face closers. Once you can communicate via text, you can improve the way you communicate effectively in every other way.

Another big benefit to closing via chat is the time. When you are on a call, you gotta wait for the rings, make the same old BS introduction, or worse yet, leave a voicemail. On top of that, as a salesman, you have to prevent any dead air on the call. You've also got to have all the answers on the fly. Finally, you can only do one sales call at a time. With chat you don't have any of those problems.

When you're using chat, you can be in the middle of several sales conversations and prospecting talks at the same time. This not only allows you to close multiple deals at once, it allows you to prospect at a much faster rate. On top of that, if you don't have the answer to a question from a prospect, you can look it up or ask about it before you answer. There's no immediate response needed.

But, there are always some of you who may say, "My prospects are not on Facebook," or "My prospects don't text." Allow me to call bullshit. Facebook has almost two billion users. A lot of your prospects are on there. Maybe not every day (probably though) but they are on there. Same with text; if you have a cell phone number, the person on the other end can text. If my grandma texts, your prospect does.

With All of That Explained, Now Let's Get to the Good Stuff.

We've all been hit with the BS message from at least one MLM person. You know the deal. They send you a message with a link that reads something like: "D*eal of a lifetime*" or "G*round floor opportunity.*" These messages don't work. They piss off way more people than you can imagine. Think of online prospecting like this: *If you don't like something done to you, don't do it to someone else.*

That includes spam.

Let's talk prospecting first. Before you can close someone, you gotta have someone to close. Facebook is full of prospects. It's the single biggest pool of prospects in one place on the planet. If you do it right, you can make a lot of sales. If you mess it up, you'll find yourself friendless and financially failing.

When Prospecting from Your Friends' List, Here's the Proper Way to Do It

First, you've got to select who you're going to prospect. Go to your friends' list and pick out the people you want to do business with. Make a list of at least 20 of them. Add them to your "must see" list and make sure you are interacting with them on their posts.

Second, look on their wall and see what they have posted lately. Have they checked in somewhere cool? Did they take a picture of someplace you know? Use what I call "social recon" to find out what they have been up to. Let's say you saw them check in at a local restaurant that you haven't been to yet. You hit them up on chat like:

"Hey man, long time no see! I was thinking about you, so I went to your wall. Looks like you're doing well. I saw that you checked in at Morton's a couple days ago. Is that place cool? Did you like the food? I've been thinking of going there."

This is a harmless message. It in NO way looks like a sales pitch. I'd estimate 99.99 percent of people on this planet operate without intent. Intent brings blame and most people don't want to be responsible for any more than they have to be. When you operate with intent paired with the right strategy, they never see it coming.

Third, after they see your message, your contact will most likely tell you all about the food and what it was like. From there, your job is to make small talk to get them warmed up. This small talk is not so small to you, though. To them, they just think it's casual conversation. To you, it's fact finding! You'll control the conversation with something like this:

"That's awesome, I'll def check it out then. How's work treating you?"

After you've talked family and life, you talk work. We Americans identify through three things: 1) where we are from, 2) our name, and 3) what we do for money. With men especially, what we do for a living is our pride. We enjoy telling others how great things are going. The prospect will probably respond with: "Work is good, how are things at your work?" That's when you hit them with this:

"My work is awesome and I can't complain. But you know how it is in the XYZ biz, I'm always looking for people who need ABCs. If you know or hear of anyone, be sure and make an intro for me. I'll do the same for you. Cool?"

It's important that you get them to agree. Don't just tell them what to do; ask them if it's okay. Even more so, ask them if it's okay following the offer to help them. That's really hard for anyone to refuse. Just like any other sales contact, most of the time they will say *"I'll keep you in mind."*, But some people might say, *"Hey man, you know what? Funny you say that. I got this…"* and you're in!

At this point, don't pounce and assume you have the sale. Just like asking questions and shutting up on a phone call or face-to-face, you'll do the same via text. Ask question after question until you get the answers you want. Once you uncover the need, simply extend an offer to help.

You may be tempted to flip a hot prospect to the phone. Only do this if THEY ask you to. If you're already chatting on Facebook, don't try to sell them on getting on the phone. The less sales you have to make to get the sale, the better. Right? Right!

I've closed hundreds of thousands of dollars in sales without ever meeting or speaking to prospects. All thanks to Facebook and Messenger. What's even better is when people message you. You can skip the BS and go straight to "W*hat made you decide to reach out?*" and get the fact-finding process rolling.

If you're looking for ways to close prospects via text, chat and email, I know how to do it. Every day I close sales from private messages. I've created a program called Show Up and Close that will teach you how it's done. Join up and in six months, you'll be a written and verbal bad ass when it comes to closing anyone anywhere. You can get the details at www.showupandclose.com.

If you're ready to invest in your personal success and you'd like to find out about the programs we

have developed especially for you, simply head over to www.HardcoreCloser.com/tribe and we'll have a sales conversation about your future.

Chapter 27

Three Ways to Word Trap a Prospect into Saying "Yes"

Sometimes you gotta trick someone into doing what's best for them. I've said it before in numerous blog posts. Humans hate making decisions because decisions come with consequences and humans lack the confidence it takes to be subjected to those consequences.

Warning! Before you read on and I take you down this path, you have to promise not to use this information to mislead or take advantage of a prospect. This strategy is to be used for good only. No evil shit. Umkay?

The great Robert Cialdini calls the principle I'm about to explain to you, the "Click Whirr" effect. In his book *Influence*, he gives an account of how his process works using door-knocking cold sales. The example he uses concerns a lady selling movie tickets. The brilliance behind the strategy is intriguing.

The saleslady shows up at the prospect's door. Instead of pitching what she's selling she simply asks, "Sir, do you like going to the movies?" Of course, the prospect says, "Yes." *Who doesn't like the movies*? From there, she goes on to ask, "And when you're at the movies do you usually order drinks and popcorn?" Again, the prospect says, "Yes." Next, she simply asks, "If you could save money on popcorn and sodas, would that entice you to go see more movies?" Again, "Yes."

With those three questions asked, she can now go in for the kill. All she has to do is simply repeat what she said using the prospect's answers and give a simple call to action. Like this: "Since you already go to movies, and each time you order popcorn and soda, I'd like to save you money. You can buy these packs of movie tickets with popcorn and soda included, at a 40 percent discount from what it costs direct from the counter. Surely, you're tired of paying exorbitant prices at the theatre and would like to save money. How many would you like to buy?"

Many of us salesmen rely on an ability to speak well to close sales. It's a huge misconception in the sales industry that you have to be a good talker to be a good closer. Actually, the opposite is true. Good investigators and good listeners make the money. Talk is cheap, even when it comes to sales.

Being a salesman is like being a detective. The prospect gives you a few clues as to what would solve their case. Your job as a salesman is to take those clues and solve their problem. In other words, you have to investigate. Investigators ask questions. They don't tell, they ask. It's your responsibility to ask for more clues until you can ask for the business.

When you watch *CSI* or any other crime drama on TV, they always interrogate the suspect. They never let him in on their thoughts or what they have up their sleeve. They ask question after question and keep stem memory on what was said. As soon as they catch the suspect slipping up, they go in for the close, intentionally trying to trap the suspect with his own words.

You can use that same strategy in sales to close more prospects. Interrogating a prospect is just like investigating a suspect, except there's no jail time or murdered bodies involved (in most cases). Let me share three simple strategies with you that will lead you to more closed sales via stuttering prospects.

#1: Ask Them Leading Questions

In the above example of the movie ticket sale, the sales lady knew the prospect liked movies. She knew because BEFORE she tried to sell him anything she asked. She asked the question for two purposes only. One: to use against the prospect later; Two: to get him to realize he regularly uses what she is selling.

If you can ask leading questions before you reveal what you are selling, you can get the prospect to easily admit they need what you are selling. They just won't know you are selling it until it's too late to back out.

#2: Get Them to Admit They Need Help Early On

As you're walking the prospect through the sales process by asking open-ended questions, the whole point is to make them aware they need some help. If they admit they need what you sell right away, you can always hit them with the "…but you said yourself that you needed my help" when the objections try and rear their ugly heads.

Taking away objections up front is an art. You've got to know your audience and why they buy what they buy AND why they should buy it from you. Asking them leading questions that get them to admit they use or need your stuff, is a surefire way to word trap someone who's trying to crawfish out of a sale.

#3: Hold Them Accountable to Their Words

After they've answered your questions and they've realized that you're about to close them, the fear of decisions and consequences will stir up inside them. These feelings manifest themselves in the form of objections. This is where it's important that you remind them of what they said and encourage them to make a good decision (for once) by working with/buying from you.

If they say, "Yeah that's a great deal," then remind them of how great it is and that they even went so far as to mention it back to you. "Sir, you must know this is perfect for you. You said so yourself earlier when I asked if you used XYZ." It's hard for a human to go against their word. It happens, but not very often. The subconscious makes it difficult to do so...unless you're a sociopath.

If you're talking too much, you're blowing sales. If you're spending time trying to convince prospects to close instead of investigating their circumstance, you're not conducting your sales job to your fullest ability. Questions lead to confessions; confessions lead to convictions aka closed sales. Just like a detective does, ask questions and anything they say can, and will be used against them in a court of closing.

If you'd like to know more about my sales process and how I'm able to confidently dish out killer advice like I did in this magnanimous blog post, you should totally check out my UIL Selling System, available only at www.inboundleadcloser.com. Stop chasing the sale and start trapping the prospect. *For their own good, of course.

If you're ready to invest in your personal success and you'd like to find out about the programs we have developed especially for you, simply head over to www.HardcoreCloser.com/tribe and we'll have a sales conversation about your future.

Chapter 28

The Amazing Power of Stealth Selling and How It Works

Stealth selling is the easiest way to close unsuspecting prospects because it keeps you from bumping heads with even the most stubborn prospects. When done properly, you don't have to talk much, just accept payment and deliver the service you sold. There's a process to it, though. And if you deviate from it, it won't work.

I'm sure you're wondering what the process is. That's exactly why I'm writing this article; to teach you. But first, let's go over some outlines and definitions. Feel like you're in grade school again? Good! Class is now in session.

Let's look at the word "stealth" for a minute. When referring to a jet, stealth means one that can fly under the radar, or that flies undetected by radar. As you and I both know, prospects have a radar. Stealth selling is the best way to stay off their radar, and to avoid setting off their bullshit meter!

It's also important that we talk about manipulation real quick before I get too deep into this. I'm trusting you to NOT use what I'm about to tell you for evil. You can't screw people over and rip them off using this. It's not cool and only d-bag losers lie and steal from prospects. Okay, now that that's out of the way.

When you're in a sales conversation, two forms of anxiety happen. On one side of the conversation, the prospect is anxious. He's anxious he might fall for a trick and get sold something he doesn't want. Even worse, he might overpay for it. This leaves his knees bouncing and his guard up.

On the other side of the conversation is the sales guy. He's nervous, too. Nervous he might say the wrong thing and blow the sale. Worried he might not get a paycheck for the effort he put in to get to this conversation. All of this anxiety and negative thinking can get in the way of a good sale.

Instead of conjuring up a conversation that causes stress, let's just avoid the whole thing and use some sales Judo on the prospect. If we fly in and sell under the radar, they'll be happier to buy from us. It sucks that it has to be this way, but it is what it is. After all, if you can't beat 'em…join 'em.

Let me give you an example of stealth selling and how easy it is to do. Yes, there's an extra one or two steps you must take to make it work, but the payout is always worth the effort. Better to take an extra couple steps and close a deal than take no steps and lose a sale.

Let's say you own a roofing business. Roofers are a dime a dozen and everyone is skeptical of them. Homeowners also know that a new roof can cost between $10,000 and $50,000 depending on what shingles they buy. Also, you have a deductible that must be paid in order to claim the new roof on insurance. Most times, the deductible is one percent of the value of the home. On a $300,000 home that's $3,000 out of the homeowner's pocket.

Naturally, when someone is about to drop three thousand bucks towards a thirty-thousand-dollar job, they might be skeptical. What's even worse is when they didn't know they needed a roof and so they start thinking the roofing salesman is full of it and just trying to get over on them. All this makes for a tough and awkward sale. To complicate matters, most roofing sales happen as a result of random door knocking in affected neighborhoods.

Let me show you an easier way to close that deal using stealth selling techniques. Instead of knocking doors, let's run an ad. Doesn't matter if it's on TV, radio, or the Internet, we just need to get the word out. The ad should read "We clean gutters for a $25 flat fee, no matter the size of your home." Most gutter cleaning services are $150 plus.

Your deal is so amazing how could a client not call you to clean their gutters? The thing is, when you go up there to clean the gutters, you are on the roof.

You can inspect the roof. Most people know if you offer a "free roof inspection" you're going to sell them roofing. They never put gutters and roof sales together.

When you finish cleaning the gutters, you go back to the front door and say, "While I was on your roof, I noticed you've got a lot of shingle damage. I can introduce you to my trusted roof guy if you want." Who's going to deny a seemingly disinterested third party who's just trying to help? No one!

The bonus part is that now, instead of you offering free roofing inspections, you get paid $25/ lead to clean the gutters and make a passing suggestion of what needs to be done. No more door knocking. No more arguing to get on the roof and most importantly no more free inspections. You now get paid up front for leads and on the back end for roofs.

In this scenario, you're able to swoop in under the prospect's sales radar, and help them get what they want in a way they are willing to accept. It's a process, but a highly effective one. Yes, there are a few steps and some outside-the-box thinking needed, but the sales are ALL there to be closed like clockwork.

This is the roofing equivalent of giving a free video then asking for a sale. The law of reciprocity plays a big factor in the process, too. Your target sees that your gutter cleaning service was so cheap, your roofing guy must be super cheap, too. They are getting a deal in their mind that you don't even know about yet. It's almost comical.

I'm a salesman by nature. It's what I do. Moreover, it's what I eat, sleep and live. I'm addicted to the intrigue of the human mind. I not only teach this stuff, I do it daily. I make sales calls and run ads every day of the week. I'm not speaking about this stuff from theory; it's from firsthand experience. If you'd like to learn more sales techniques like the one in this article, check out my sales program Show Up and Close at www.showupandclose.com.

If you're ready to invest in your personal success and you'd like to find out about the programs we have developed especially for you, simply head over to www.HardcoreCloser.com/tribe and we'll have a sales conversation about your future.

Chapter 29

How to Psych Yourself Out of a Sales Slump

Nothing is worse in our industry than when you're in a dry spell. If you're not careful, it can creep up on you and leave you broke AF. Dry spells kill our confidence. We become fearful of losing the next sale, knowing we need to close it more than any sale before in our career. That's a lot of self-pressure and it rarely works.

Dry slumps are all in your head. Sales is a numbers game. You've got to get in front of 100 people to close one. Unless you're me, then you need to get in front of 1,000 to close one (ISO the elite only). Most of the time, the numbers stay consistent. You talk to 100 people, one buys. Sometimes though, you go through 300 without a single show of interest.

Much like other droughts, sales droughts can end with floods, too. Patience always pays off. When you bust through those 300 without a sale, chances are in the next 100, you'll hit three closes in a row. UNLESS, you let it get to your head. If the drought gets to your head, you may make 1,000 calls or more before you snap out of it…and that's if you snap out of it at all.

How Can You Avoid Getting Sucked into an Inescapable Sales Slump?

Like I was saying above, sales is all about numbers. There's no algorithm. These are random lotto type numbers. There's not a salesman on the planet who doesn't already know this. So then, why do they let slumps affect them when really there's no such thing as a slump?

Human emotions are some powerful things. After all, the most influential object on earth is the human mind. Emotions are manufactured by our limitless brains. Emotions will almost always interfere with rationality. Even though WE KNOW it's a numbers game, we tend to talk in slumps and lose self-confidence. If we want out, all we need to do is keep hitting numbers.

The best salesmen have learned to avoid emotion and push on no matter what. We listen to motivational speeches, jam music, read books, do drugs and whatever else we can indulge in to avoid emotions. Emotions can cost commissions. Who cares if they say "No!" or don't buy? There's another prospect in line right after them.

With a sucker born every second, no matter what you sell, you'll eventually close a deal. It's your job to relentlessly seek that deal and not be affected by all the "be backs", "nos" and "looky-loos" you'll run across.

Now that I've clearly explained to you what a slump is, how it's caused and why we fall into them, let's talk about getting out of one when you're sucked in. It happens to all of us. We ALL go through dry spells. The cards/numbers don't always get dealt in the right order.

How Can You Drag Yourself Out of a Sales Slump Once You're in Deep?

I've hit a few dry spells in my day. They usually come at the worse times, like when you're on a new job, or an unexpected bill shows up. Combine seemingly already stressful situations with a lack of closings and a guy like me will lose his cool. Once the cool is lost, it's hard to get back.

These days, I'm proactive and I try to keep "the cool" at all times. I make sure that if I'm in a "slump" I don't let emotions keep me there. In order to pull this off, you gotta be super self-aware. You've got to be a master of your own mind. Your mind can make or break a slump with one decision.

Back in the day, when I'd hit dry spells and lose confidence in myself just like anyone else, the first thing I'd do was try to become aware. When I started bitching about not closing deals, I'd catch myself and at that point realize the slump was creeping. Just like any other problem, if you don't know it exists, you can't solve it.

The next thing I'd do, once aware, was preserve my confidence. The key to closing is confidence. If you lose it, you lose sales. It's that simple. How I held onto confidence even though my morale was getting murdered was easy. I just remembered the last five or six clients I'd closed. I remembered how happy they were and what results I'd gotten for them. That kind of reminiscing is always a good reminder of why we grind on.

It may sound cheesy, but I'd hit the books and YouTube, too if I caught myself in a slump. I'd watch motivational sales videos before work and listen to audio books about sales. If what I was doing wasn't making sales, I was determined to listen to content that could help me change that. It's always an amazing thing to see one line, one sentence, or even one word that can change the game for us salesmen.

If you can't surround yourself with greatness, don't settle for mediocrity. Meaning, if you're the top guy and you're in a slump, don't resort to joining Harold from three cubes over and griping about the leads. It's never the leads. It's always on us. There's a reason Harold sucks. Don't hang with losers.

To take it one step further, you can call past clients

and ask them how they are doing and what results they have obtained through using your stuff. Those testimonials can arm you with word tracks to use in your next meeting. Plus, hearing happy clients will open up your mind and restore confidence in what you're selling again.

Let's recap. You gotta be aware. Knowing you're hitting the wall is the first step. Then you've got to restore confidence by calling or thinking about success stories you've created. After that, get some motivation. Music, videos, books, or whatever it is; just get it and channel it into sales.

On a side note, what I also like to do is hit the gym hard. If I can break records with my body and push it to the limit, I can get my confidence back. Feeling cocky about a workout can get you back to being cocky at work. Also, exhausting your body can give you mental clarity and realign your direction. Some of my clearest thoughts have come from hard workouts. Those thoughts have cured many a sales "slump."

Education is important, too. Just as videos and books can break you out, the same can be said for training programs. The more you educate yourself, the more sales you make...as long as you take action. I've got a program packed full of motivation and the information needed to bust anyone out of a sales slump. You can check it out here at www.inboundleadcloser.com.

If you're ready to invest in your personal success and you'd like to find out about the programs we have developed especially for you, simply head over to www.HardcoreCloser.com/tribe and we'll have a sales conversation about your future.

Chapter 30

The Greatest Sales Lesson You'll Ever Learn

Alright, class is in session. I'll be your instructor and I expect your full attention as I embark on today's amazing lesson in sales. I warn you, DO NOT discredit the information you're about to read or the teacher of said lesson. Let's get into it, shall we?

Some of the best information is overlooked due to its simplicity. For some weird reason, people are quick to discredit stuff that is easy. Weird thing is, systems don't have to be complicated or confusing in order to work. Matter of fact, the exact opposite is the truth. Yet many people fail to win due to discrediting simplicity.

Before I get into the lesson, I need you to take your "simplicity discrediting" judgment hat off. If you don't, you'll miss the power behind this message. You'll also miss out on all the money you can make from implementing the information you're about to learn.

The power of simplicity can be broken down into an element everyone understands and misunderstands at the same time. I've seen smart salesmen fail at their jobs and get outsold by guys with mid-level intelligence due to the fact the "dumb guys" did and said what they were told.

There's no need to reinvent the wheel in sales. What worked 1,000 years ago, still works today. Methods are many; principles are few; methods may vary, but principles never do. IDK who originally said that, but it for sure applies to the sales industry.

I've not even gotten into the real message of this post yet, and you've already learned a powerful lesson. One that pairs with what I'm about to share. You see, you and I may be smart, but we are the one percent. We sell to the other 99 percent. They need simplicity. We should give it to them, and then we should sell them our stuff.

With all that said, I'll now share with you one sentence that will ALWAYS be the greatest sales lesson you'll ever learn (assuming you embrace it.)

Sell Them What They Want to Be Sold

It really is that easy. As I stated earlier, most sales people don't close as much as they can because they complicate things. The average client needs information delivered to them in a simple fashion. In most cases, they don't know or care about what all goes into what you sell, they care about the result they need your product to produce for them.

Allow me to be perfectly clear with you. No matter what your boss, trainer, manager, or mentor tells you, no one is buying you. They are buying what you sell. They buy from you because you are the roadblock between what they want and getting it.

People buy what they want to buy. The salesman who can best demonstrate how what he sells can solve the problem of the prospect is ALWAYS the one who wins the business. I've never had the pleasure of selling anything that was the cheapest. Every job I've ever had in sales was always selling a product or service way more expensive than the "competition."

In the beginning, I was naive enough to think it was about me. I literally thought people paid more for my cars/mortgages and stuff because they liked me. While they may have liked me, they bought because I sold them what they were looking for.

No consumer wants to deal with you. They want what you sell and whether you want to admit it or not, as a salesman, you're simply an obstacle on the road to getting what they want. The sooner you know this and act accordingly, the sooner your bank account will thank you.

That doesn't mean some of us can't talk our way into a sale. We can sell ourselves to prospects all day long and eventually some of them will buy from us.

We can also shut up about us and talk more about what they want. By doing this, I PROMISE you, your closing ratios will increase.

Let me put it this way:

- *No one wants a real estate agent or mortgage*—they want a home—sell the home.

- *No one wants a car salesman with good service*—they want a ride that fits their lifestyle—sell the car.

- *No one wants a business consultant*—they want more clients, time and/or money—sell the results.

- *No one wants life insurance*—they want peace of mind—sell them a worry-free future.

The sooner you stop selling you, your company and all that other BS and you start selling what they want, you'll make more money. After all, more money is what you want, right? It's why you do this job. So, why not maximize every turn you get with a prospect with the fullest ability to close?

If you don't know what your prospects want, you're a horrible salesman. There I said it. If you haven't been listening to the objections, concerns and issues of your prospects to know EXACTLY what it is they want, you're failing as a salesperson.

Our job is to uncover a need and use what we sell to fulfill that need. Nothing more. Nothing less. Notice I didn't say our job is to show the client why they should buy from us and our company. The only thing tying their need to our company is that they have to go through us to get their need fulfilled.

No consumer ever, ever, ever in a million years will roll over in the middle of the night, wake their spouse up and say, "We need to find a place with a great salesman and excellent service to buy XYZ." That's not how it works. They roll over and say, "I'm pregnant, we need a new house." "They say, "We've got to figure out a way to save money so we can pay off our credit cards."

Again, don't discredit what I'm saying here due to simplicity. Most of us didn't go to, or graduate from some Ivy League school. Most of the information we learned in our educational days has been forgotten anyway. Try not to overcomplicate stuff. One of the most popular subreddits is the "Explain Like I'm Five" page. People like simple stuff. Oblige them.

I could go on forever about this, but then I'd only make it more complicated for you which would make me a hypocrite, which I'm not. So, I'll leave you with this: if you don't already know (shame on you) what it is your prospects really want, you need to listen more and uncover it.

I learned early on in my consulting business that people didn't want a business consultant. The egotistical Alpha males I work with don't want to admit they need help with anything. What they do want is more time off (systems) or more leads (funnels). Nothing more, nothing less. When I talk to a prospect, all I'm trying to do is find out which one it is for them, and then sell them what they want. I never talk about me or my background. Who the hell cares?

You may not know this, but I teach people kickass lessons like this in my sales training program called Show Up and Close. If you're looking for more leads, higher close ratios and killer sales training, this is the program that will deliver larger commission checks to you (assuming you do what I teach you). You can check out the first few trainings free of charge at www.showupandclose.com.

If you're ready to invest in your personal success and you'd like to find out about the programs we have developed especially for you, simply head over to www.HardcoreCloser.com/tribe and we'll have a sales conversation about your future.

Chapter 31

Overcoming the "Let Me Talk to My Partner" Objection in Three Steps

If there's one objection I think salesmen get the most, it's "Let me talk to my partner." It's almost as bad as being put in the friend zone with a chick you dig. I don't know a single salesman possessing 12 months or more experience, who's not had this zinger thrown at them at least once.

What Can You Do to Close Over the "Talk to My Partner" Objection?

It's a question I get every time I do a Q&A. It also comes up in my Sales Talk With Sales Pros group often. As you know, every sales situation is unique. What works in one scenario may not work in the next. Sales is a fluid practice of daily adaptation.

The main problem with this objection is that it usually comes out of nowhere from people who don't need to talk to anyone. It's simply a stall tactic from a person who's afraid to make a decision OR who thinks your sales game is weak.

The sooner you start looking at ALL objections like this, the faster your paychecks will grow. Every great salesman knows that removing as many emotions as you can out of the process is the key. The more you can respond to objections and stall tactics on mental autopilot, the more sales you'll make.

Getting Emotionally Wrapped Up in Objections Kills Your Sales Game

Prospects often resort to throwing the "Let me ask my partner" objection as the last-ditch effort to blame someone other than themselves for trying to get out of the deal. While this is not always the case, it's the case more often than not. The best way to close over this objection is to take the wind out of their sails as soon as you can.

Here's how I handle the partner objection as soon as it comes up. It's better to blow a sale five minutes in than to spend hours with someone only to find out they weren't serious about buying anyway. I like to know what I'm dealing with BEFORE I get on the phone or meet someone.

Step #1:

Ask before they get on the call if there will be another decision maker involved. Let them know this is a serious decision to be made and if they have a partner, spouse, boss, or assistant who needs to hear it, get that addressed up front. I get real businesslike and say, "If we are going to talk serious business, let's get serious. Is there anyone else you'll need to consult in our meeting in order to make a yes or no decision?"

Asking up front is fun for us salespeople because when that prospect says, "Well, I have a partner, but he can't make it. I'll relay the info to him." You can ask them, "Are you authorized by your partner to make a decision or do you need their blessing?" If they need the blessing, suggest scheduling another time with them both, so no one has to repeat the time spent.

Step #2:

Offer to get on the phone, too and answer their partner's questions just like you did for them. Sometimes they'll tell you they don't have a partner and then throw one at you outta nowhere. You know how it is, buyers are liars. When they bring this up on you, don't get mad or try and point out that they lied. That's ego, not sales.

If this happens to you, simply look directly at them and say "Great, we can call them now and since I'm right here, I'll answer all of their questions for you." At that point, you'll usually find out if they are time-wasting tire kickers or serious. I've had plenty of people get on the phone right in front of me and hand it off to me.

Step #3:

Give it to them straight. If they insist on leaving to talk to their partner, that's when you know there's a 99 percent chance of them turning into a ghost. Here's what I say to them when this happens, "I'll just shoot you straight. If you're serious and YOU think this is what the best decision is, you need to make it. Your partner is not here. They didn't get the experience or have the same desires as you. All they are going to do is talk you out of it. I see it happen all the time. Let me help you get what you want by making a decision today." It's hard to argue with that.

The one thing many salesmen lack is brutal honesty. The more you can address issues up front the less issues you'll have on the close. No matter who they are, prospects appreciate a confident salesman who isn't afraid to ask the hard questions. Asking hard questions shows you have no fear *and* that you have all the answers.

Like I said to begin with, all sales scenarios are different. I've closed a sale before by saying, "I'm looking at your credit; you've made bad decisions all your life, why don't you make a good one for a change and go with my advice?" It's a ballsy thing to tell them, but in that moment the dude needed to hear it.

If you're a good salesman, you can add a few items to your sales soldier armory to turn you from a good closer to a legend—one future sales dudes in your place will hear about when they get hired. I've got the tools to make it happen. I can actually put you together every day before work when you use my www.showupandclose.com program. It's designed for you to listen to one audio every day before you hit the sales streets. I've even included a few free videos.

If you're ready to invest in your personal success and you'd like to find out about the programs we have developed especially for you, simply head over to www.HardcoreCloser.com/tribe and we'll have a sales conversation about your future.

Chapter 32

Six Reasons You're Blowing Sales and Losing Money

I don't know about you, but when I blow a sale, I want to kick myself in the nuts. The only upside to losing a sale is the lesson learned from it. I'm not trying to learn too much, though, if you catch my drift.

When I started off selling, I didn't have someone pointing out the holes in my game. I, much like you probably did, learned my stuff from taking action, reading books and trying new stuff I had seen others use successfully. It made for a long learning cycle, that's for sure. Allow me to shorten it for you.

Oftentimes, as salesmen, we will know something but simply forget it. How many times have you heard an old school close and thought *man, I forgot about that, I need to start using it again*? It happens all the time. We get caught up in the game and simply forget.

If you're blowing sales, there are usually some fundamental issues you're not addressing properly and all it takes is a reminder paired with action. Here are the top six reasons people blow sales. Remember it this time!

#1: You Talk Too Much

Shut up! No, seriously. Sometimes all a salesman needs to do to close is shut the F up. You have no clue how many times I've watched a salesman talk his way OUT of a sale. I've seen it with my own eyes. The prospect wants to buy and the damn salesman says too much.

Decisions cause collisions. The more options you give someone, the less likely they are to make a choice. This prolongs the sale with objections like "Lemme think about it." People need to be led to the choice that's best for them. You can't do that if you're talking too much.

#2: You're Over-Promising and They Know It

Ever get that *it's too good to be true* feeling? Yeah, so do your prospects when you're laying the BS on too thick. If you can't do it, don't say it. They will most likely accept things the way they are. You don't have to offer the imaginary.

When you say something you know you can't do, your body puts off a vibe. The prospect can feel that vibe in your body language through a phone line. Just tell it like it is and show them why they need what you sell. Drop the BS. It only comes back to bite you in the end anyway.

#3: You Make It About You and Not Them

The prospect doesn't care about you or your background. What they do care about is how what you sell can solve their problem. What is it with salesmen who think they need to give you their background? This isn't a dating profile. It's a sales conversation. Unless you are what's for sale, talk about what you sell, not who's selling it.

The prospect cares about what your products or services can do for them, not what you can do for them. Matter of fact, the less you talk about what you can do, the less they'll ask you to do it. It's a win/win for everyone. You're a nobody. Your product is the hero.

#4: You Quit On the First Objection

The first objection is always a test, and 99 percent of salesmen fail it. Most sales guys just accept the first "no" thrown out in the process. The first "no" is merely a test to see how much you are willing to do to make the sale. If you quit in the sale, chances are you'll quit in the delivery. They can smell it a mile away.

Just like you have trial closes, customers have trial objections. All they are doing is testing the waters and seeing how you'll react. Knowing this and removing emotions like fear from the conversation will close more sales and give you nuts like King Kong.

#5: You Believe Their BS (Buyers are Liars)

We lie to ourselves on a daily basis. What makes you think buyers aren't lying to themselves when they say, "I didn't come to buy today." Just take a minute to think about the BS stories we tell ourselves every day. Your prospects are the same. They have the same stupid self-limiting beliefs most everyone has.

If you know what you sell will help them, it's your job to sort through the noise in their head and give them clarity about why they should buy, why they deserve it and how it will positively impact them. Don't let their lies cost you money,

#6: You Don't Properly Ask for the Business

Sometimes, simply asking for the business will get it. Problem is many salesmen think they asked for it, but in the prospect's mind they are left hanging. Saying you'll follow up, call them, or reach out is not asking for business. When you make an offer you need to clearly articulate the terms.

The keys to making a clear offer are as follows: 1) verbalize it, 2) put it on paper, and 3) get it signed. If you follow these steps to making an offer, you'll get a direct "NO" or a "YES." That's all we want in this game—a clear answer.

Okay, now that you've been refreshed on why you're not getting all you can get, when are you going to implement these methods back into your business? I didn't write this for my help, I wrote it so cool-ass people like you will read it and put it into play in their everyday sales lives.

If you'd like more help on your sales game, I've got the prescription for you. I've created a program where you'll to listen to one audio a day, every day for the rest of your career. You'll become a machine through repetition. Here's the site to check it out and even get a free video: www.showupandclose.com.

If you're ready to invest in your personal success and you'd like to find out about the programs we have developed especially for you, simply head over to www.HardcoreCloser.com/tribe and we'll have a sales conversation about your future.

Chapter 33

Five Steps You Must Walk Every Prospect Through in Order to Close

The best salesmen I know have selling systems in place. They use these selling systems to remove their emotions from the selling equation. They follow their systems to a T, too. Just like soldiers doing rifle drills blindfolded, the best salesmen have a process they could do blindfolded.

I remember when I was a "good" salesman and thinking I had it going on. I could overcome objections, give witty responses and close deals. Then one day, I hired a mentor and he put me together. Meaning, he gave me a system to go with my selling, instead of the method I had been using: me, just grasping at random closing techniques. *I can honestly say it changed the game for me.*

Removing the emotion from the salesman side of the sales conversation is a huge advantage. Again, just like soldiers who are trained to pull the trigger without thinking or emotion, salesmen can be armed in the same way with words.

Once I learned this simple 5-step process, my closing ratios went up and my sales calls flowed more smoothly. Using this technique ends up being a better experience for the prospect, too. Everybody feels great about the process and everyone wins when you close in this manner. You can't beat it.

Having a Proven Sales System in Place Will Turn a Good Salesman into a BAMF Closer

I'll share with you the five phases every sales conversation must go through in order to close. It's fair to mention there's a million ways to spin this, so I'm not going to take all of your time over elaborating. Remember, the simpler things are, the more likely they are to work.

#1: Bonding

This is the first phase you must enter when you start the sales process. It's the easiest phase to complete, but it is not to be skipped or ignored. This is where you show the prospect they are a lot like you or a lot like others you've helped.

People identify with three main things. 1) where they are from, 2) their name, and 3) what they do for a living. These are usually the three most important identifying factors for a person. Asking where they live and knowing someone in that town or city, or having been there yourself helps. Addressing the prospect by name is also a bonus. If you can share a story they like or get them to laugh, you're golden.

#2: Trust

You've gotten them to bond with you and like you, now they need to know you're not full of shit. Anyone can easily tell a story and relate to someone, but what about earning enough trust to get them to open their wallet? It's as easy as social proof.

Social proof happens when you show the prospect examples and testimonials of past and current clients who've achieved what the current prospect wants. When they see others, especially people they know, who've obtained what they want, they will let their guard down. Show them how you've helped others.

#3: Interest

Now that they like you, trust you and know you, you need them interested in your product. During the previous phase, you showed them social proof examples of results they want. Now it's time to explain to them how they, too can get the same results using your products.

They now see what's possible and are most likely visualizing themselves experiencing those results. They want it. It's just a matter of knowing the details. This is where you don't talk numbers, but you talk benefits and ONLY those benefits that will matter to the prospect.

#4: Desire

They've seen results and have become interested in what you have, and now they have a reason to buy. That reason could be saving money, beating the competition, cutting down on overhead, or time efficiency. Your job is to keep asking questions and fact-finding until you build their desire.

When they start asking you how much it costs or how long until they can get it, you know you got 'em. Those phrases are buying signs which mean they have a craving to purchase (assuming it all works out in the numbers world.)

#5: Offer

This is the most important part of the process, because after all, it's the close. Sure you can use little trial closes along the way before you make the offer, but unless you've completed the four previous steps, your offer won't be seriously considered.

Once you have heightened the desire, so they want what you have, it's your job to perfectly present the offer to them in a manner they can't refuse. As soon as you make the offer, ask them, "What's next?" This keeps any awkward silence from occurring after the offer, as well as it allows the momentum to continue to flow.

Before you get on your next sales call, print out this shit and keep it at your desk. As you make your calls, go through the 5-step checklist and don't move on until you're SURE you've completed each phase. In doing this, you will watch your normal emotions go out the door.

Once your emotions are gone and you have a system you can trust in place, your closing ratios will skyrocket, your prospects will give you better treatment and you will close more sales. I didn't believe it either, until I just did it. Next thing I knew, I had people like you reading blog posts like this.

If you're looking to step up your sales in a major way, put a selling system in place that's proven to work and one which you can practice every day, take a look at the free video I've made for you at www.showupandclose.com.

If you're ready to invest in your personal success and you'd like to find out about the programs we have developed especially for you, simply head over to www.HardcoreCloser.com/tribe and we'll have a sales conversation about your future.

Chapter 34

Seven Hardcore Closes That Save Sales and Seal Deals

We all want to close more sales. Right? I mean, if you're in the sales industry and your goal this month is not bigger than the goal you set for last month, you're in the wrong industry. Maybe you should try being an interior decorator or a scientist.

For those of us with serious goals on our mind, the only way we can hit those goals is by simply closing more sales. In order to close more sales, not only do you need more prospects, you also need better calls to action, so you can make the most out of the prospects you pitch.

The best closes are simple but bold. They consist of word tracks the average salesman is afraid to mutter. Closes that convert contain confidence. When you're able to say what others won't, you'll close what others don't.

I've put together my seven favorite, go-to word tracks that get the job done. I've personally recited these closes thousands of times each. I spit them out from muscle memory these days. If you'll memorize and use them in your everyday closing convos, you'll see the difference, too.

#1: Take Away Close

"You're number one on my list, but since you turned me down I am going to work with John Smith now. Do you know him?"

Most people view take away closes as "you can't have it" BS. I do mine a little differently. When a prospect says they are not interested, try the shit I'm about to share with you. It works. Before you have the meeting, do your research. Find out your prospect's competitor's name. As soon as they say, "No," simply tell them it's a damn shame you're going to have to do this stuff for (insert competitor's name.)

#2: Hey, By the Way

"Hey by the way, this is what I do. If you like this and want more help with it, I can help you, but I want your business in exchange. What's it gonna be?"

Passively selling can be extremely effective if used correctly. This sale works best when you are creating the bond and trust. When the small talk is gone and the offer needs to be made, this method can be one of the most effective, yet one of the easiest phrases to throw out.

#3: If Not You, Who?

"I understand you are not interested, so who do you know who will be? I'm going to make an example out of someone. If it's not you, who would you like to see me help?"

Sometimes, you get turned down. The prospect huffs their chest and just says, "NO." Most people expect you to just take their "NO" and leave, but not you. You're gonna thank them for their time and ask who they know who you can help. Most people will give you referrals just so you'll not ask them for biz again. #winning

#4: Lead by Example

"This is what worked for the last agent when they did business with me. If you would like those same results for you, cool. If not, I'll be on my way." (Make sure you have prepared the results in advance).

If you have the ability to show your stuff working for someone else, especially if that someone else is an authority figure in the market, you'll land more deals, plain and simple. Lots of people just talk and make noise. If you come armed with real life examples of success, it's going to make it harder for that prospect to say, "NO."

#5: You Want It, Don't You?

"I closed three deals from social media last month. Surely, your friends want to do business with you, right?"

This gem includes one of the strongest elements of influence there is—social proof. Showing the prospect other people similar to them who have obtained the results they want will make a competitive person think they can do it, too. That's when you get 'em!

#6: I Know, But

"I know you're loyal, but do you want to grow your business or do you want to continue to feed theirs?"

No matter what is said, it is all voided by what comes after the "but." This is the close you go to when they tell you they already have a relationship with another vendor in place. If what you sell is better for them or their clients, why wouldn't they want to push your stuff on the same terms?

#7: What's Next

"Absolutely I'd love to make that happen for you, what's next?"

Action words get deals closed. Nothing is worse than playing the He-Who-Speaks-First-Loses game when you've just made an offer. Instead, try what I do, keep the momentum flowing by making the pitch then asking them to make a decision. Simple. Bold. Effective.

I've recorded a free sales audio for you to listen to in traffic or in the gym that will lead you to more closed sales. Download it here and change your life: http://bit.ly/2cTiDVd

If you're ready to invest in your personal success and you'd like to find out about the programs we have developed especially for you, simply head over to www.HardcoreCloser.com/tribe and we'll have a sales conversation about your future.

Chapter 35

Seven Word Tracks You Can Use to Overcome Prospect Objections

As a lifelong student of the sales game, I'm always arming myself, my sales team and my clients with word tracks, that if memorized and used correctly, can help when you are in heated sales negotiations to overcome prospect objections.

The key with word tracks is to not only memorize them, but to use them on a regular basis. If you do phone, car, or real estate sales and you find yourself needing a quick comeback for an objection, a word track can save you in a pinch.

Remember flash cards in school? Think of word tracks like flashcards. The faster you get at firing them out, the more sales you can close.

I've come up with seven of the best word tracks I know. These are my personal go-to closes that I use regularly. Yes, they may seem simple and that's exactly why they work. The less complicated you make the sale, the better.

Word Track #1:

"I completely understand where you are coming

from, sign here."

Sounds too easy huh? Truth is, this word track works more often than you'd expect. It takes confidence to look a prospect in the eye right after they've handed you a bullshit objection…and still close them.

This close is not for the weak. Oftentimes, the prospect just wants to feel your confidence in getting the job done. Using this word track usually opens the prospect's mind to the foolishness of their objection.

Word Track #2:

"One day you're going to go from just looking to buying anyway. Let me save you the time and turn you into a client today. Let's roll!"

The "let's roll" on the end of this word track is crucial. It keeps the momentum and energy flowing. Look, they wouldn't be checking out what you sell if they didn't like it. Why people deprive themselves in the ways they do, I'll never understand.

Your prospect is most likely going to buy what you sell in the near future anyway, why not make them a buyer today? This will not only free up their time due to no more looking around, but it will give them the happiness of ownership.

Word Track #3:

"You can absolutely talk to your spouse. Would you like to use my office phone?"

Oh God, they hate it when you call their bluff and pull this one on them. Even worse is when they say, "I'll talk to her at home we need privacy" I always comeback with "Privacy? No problem, you can use my office."

Most of the time the spouse knows their partner is shopping and has already given the go-ahead. The spouse objection is simply a stall tactic. Don't fall for it. Remember, closing is a service. It's a favor to the prospect.

Word Track #4:

"I like where your head's at and the numbers you came up with, but this is a real deal and the best one I can give you. Sign here."

People always have lower numbers in their head than what's real (thanks largely to lies on the Internet.) They forget taxes, fees and whatever else they don't take into account when they come up with their estimate. Then they always act shocked when your numbers, the real numbers, are higher than the mystical guesstimate they made up.

It's your job as a salesman to show them the math and get them to understand that the numbers they have dreamed up are wrong…in a cool way, of course. Be calm, do the math and build value to show them it's worth the cost.

Word Track #5:

"I'd say the same thing if I were in your position, but we can get all this done now and stop prolonging the pain. What's next?"

The "what's next" is a big part of this. Again, it keeps the momentum up. When you overcome a big objection by using this word track, you've got to keep them moving or they might get offended.

This close can be used when the prospect has a lower expectation of price than what the price really is. Simply agree with them that you'd want that deal too, and then show them why it's a good idea to buy today.

Word Track #6:

"My job is to make sure you're happy with your purchase. I take my job very seriously. What can I do to make you happy today?"

Good customer service can really help close a sale. The law of reciprocity is strong if you go above and beyond. Now, of course, there are always sociopaths who don't care, but the majority of people will appreciate being treated right.

This close will also let you know what the prospect's expectations are, assuming they tell you what would make them close. Even if their numbers or wants are way the F off, keep working them toward the middle and show them you're on their team.

Word Track #7:

"You can't lose. The consequences of this decision can only bring happiness to your life. You do deserve to be happy don't you?"

A good deal is a good deal. If you know you're giving them a great deal, they know you're giving them a great deal, just f'n close it, will you!!! If you're attempting to close on a win-win or a win in the client's direction, don't be afraid to show them why they are winning.

People love to feel like they got over on a salesman. I learned early on to exploit this and make them think I didn't know what they were doing. Meanwhile I'd always be two steps ahead. People love to win, show them a win, then close them!

Now that you've got some new word tracks to use in these everyday objective situations, use them.

They won't do you any good if you don't move your lips and say them to living breathing prospects.

Again, I know they may be simple, but keeping it simple keeps it selling. Trust me on that. Simplicity sells. That's why superhero movies sell and documentaries don't. Simple. Sadly, most folks are simple, but that's what they need anyway, so it all works out.

If you're looking to step up your sales game with word tracks, strategies and methods that will enable you to close more deals, my Show Up and Close program will change your life. Seriously, I'll even give you some free videos in advance to prove it. Simply go to www.showupandclose.com.

If you're ready to invest in your personal success and you'd like to find out about the programs we have developed especially for you, simply head over to www.HardcoreCloser.com/tribe and we'll have a sales conversation about your future.

Chapter 36

The Psychology Behind Being a Solid Salesman

Ever see a successful salesman who didn't have much of a personality? What about a quiet sales guy? Although they are a strange phenomenon, there are serious reasons why they are a closer without the typical closer persona.

We have this inner perception of what a salesman looks, acts and talks like. Often, that perception is wrong. Some of the most powerful closers I know are quiet, humble and caring people who've genuinely mastered their craft in order to better serve those in need.

That's what it's really all about anyway. Being the best salesman you can, in order to close those who need your services the most.

According to what we've learned in school, we have five senses. However, recently I read an article that claimed we really have *nine* senses. One of those nine senses? Intuition.

Intuition means we have a deep-down unfounded reason to believe or simply know that something is right for us. The problem is, most of us have stopped trusting our gut. It's funny, the millions of times in your life that your gut has helped you, can all be halted by the one time it is wrong.

This halting keeps humans from having the desire to make a decision. Because, once a decision is made, the person who made it has to live with the consequences. Good or bad.

A good salesman knows this up front. He's prepared to deal with objections, anxiety and even anger from the prospect at times. A closer knows when to listen, when to speak and when to offer empathy.

Empathy plays a huge part in the process of being a killer closer because you have to understand the apprehensions of your prospects. A closer knows that the sale is never going to be a lay down.

Understanding the issues and objections your prospects have up front, and having empathy for them; moreover, having the ability to demonstrate genuine empathy, will get more deals closed, no matter your personality type.

On top of empathy, a solid salesman will also need a massive amount of patience. The more a salesman listens, the more the chances of making the sale increase. The more a salesman talks, the less likely he is to close.

How Can You Close a Sale, if You Didn't Listen to the Problem?

Most salesmen assume they know what's best for the client. While they may know what's best, they often don't try to uncover the "why" behind it. Every buyer has their own personal motivation. The sooner you learn how to uncover their "why," the more sales you will make.

Prospects can get mean and mad, too. When being forced to make a decision, even one they know they need to make, frustrations get high. A sharp salesman knows to keep cool and press on. The less emotion on our end toward the prospect, the better.

Let the prospect release their emotions. All you need to do is simply absorb those emotions and not let them get to you. This is why so many salespeople hate the phone. If the prospect's emotions go sideways, most salesmen follow suit.

Here's the breakdown and recap: you're gonna need confidence, empathy, knowledge, patience and the ability to play on the intuition of the prospect.

With these skills and abilities, you'll be able to connect and close more sales than you have in the past. It's these skills that will allow a master salesman to prosper even though he or she may not fit the typical salesy mold.

In order to be a closer, you don't have to talk fast, walk with a swagger, or be an asshole willing to say things others won't. These traits will work in some cases, but will most likely hurt more than they ever help.

When I was younger I'd see guys making tons of sales and think to myself, *that guys sucks, how in the hell is he closing deals like this*? But the truth is, I sucked. I had the picture in my head of a fast talker who could argue their way into a sale. That, my friends, is called doing things the hard way.

These days, I'm experienced enough to know the EXACT steps it takes to close a sale. It doesn't matter your looks, your personality, or anything else. It's all about following a formula that leads to a closed sale or a no-sale.

If you're interested in uncovering my formula for yourself and becoming the salesman you know you should be, I've got help for you. Just go to www.showupandclose.com and you'll find my "Selling with 6 C's" video series for free, which outlines the six solid steps every salesperson needs to know to close more sales. I created it to help people like you advance to the next level of selling.

If you're looking to step up your sales game with

word tracks, strategies and methods that will enable you to close more, my Show Up and **Close** program will change your life. Seriously, I'll even give you some free videos in advance to prove it. Simply go to www.showupandclose.com.

It takes daily practice and implementation to master this craft. You'll never be the best salesman if you're not talking to prospects every day and practicing your craft. Know-it-alls die rich in knowledge, but poor in action.